WHICH EVE ARE YOU

ELLEN WARD

Printed in the United States of America.

First Printed in March 10, 2024

ISBN: 978-1-956544-62-6

Printed by Amazon.com

www.BetweenFriendsPublishing.com

DEDICATION

This book is dedicated to the Master of the Universe who is never too busy to answer my questions or to stop by for a hug.

PREFACE

*"For now, there is no Jew nor Greek....no male
nor female but all are one in Christ Jesus."*

GAL 3:28

CONTENTS

INTRODUCTION

The Alpha and Omega, where the lines of the beginning and the end meet makes a circle. Is God taking us back to the beginning?

God told me more than thirty years ago that I am a King and Priest after the order of Melchizedek (Gen 14:18, Rev 1:6, 5:10). He challenged me to ask Him if this is so even for a female? You may be surprised by His answer just as I was.

CHAPTER I

IN THE BEGINNING GOD MADE US ONE, THEN TWO, THEN MORE

A. THE NARRATIVE OF ADAM AND EVE

In the beginning God created the heavens and the earth (Gen 1:1) and God said, *"Let US make man in our image after our likeness (Gen 1:26)."* Very often when we read words, we inject our understanding into words rather than letting the words reshape or reorder our thinking to define what really is being said. This is hard for us not to do because at the most fundamental core of our being, we only know that we exist first then we learn that there is a whole world around us. We begin as our own universe. So, the meaning of words or ideas can only stem from what we understand so far. Because of this, after a while, when we have read words over and over or heard them preached over and over, we remake the meaning or even the idea of God, into our limited understanding or rather into our broken or incomplete image of ourselves and the worlds

1

around us.

I invite you to listen, really listen to what these words, God has inspired to be written in His book, the Book, The Bible, are saying, especially to Eve. See if you can now recognize what has been there all along. I didn't see these concepts until God explained them to me. As far as I can remember, I have never heard this message, I'm about to share, preached anywhere. I've heard parts of it expounded but never a cohesive message that allowed anyone to describe Eve's plight as it truly is.

I also invite you not to just believe what I have written, but research it to prove out what I have written. Look up the scripture references I note! In other words, study to show yourself approved of God (2 Tim 2:15). Be sure that you know for yourself what the Book says.

The words in the Bible create a picture, a story, a narrative (if you will) of what has happened, what is happening and what will happen according to God's plan. How do I know this? I know because God said through His word, that He would do nothing without revealing His intentions to us (Duet 29:29). Do you believe Him?

Yes, some of the narrative or story is hidden and belongs only to God (Amos 3:7, Psa. 25:14, Mat 13:35) but what is revealed to us not only belongs to us but it becomes our responsibility to know and understand how the information fits into the story or narrative and consequently, into our lives. This will in turn show us how we fit into the narrative. God rewards our diligence because seeking out this knowledge is a necessary part of our existence (Heb 11:6). What is the reward for this diligence? While there are many rewards, the most needful reward is to *"enter into His rest"* (Heb 4:10) or peace of mind. This, of course, comes after accepting Jesus as Lord and Savior. Giving us the capability and a stable and strong foundation to stand on; making the most challenging of life's situations bearable (Eph 6:13).

Why must we struggle for knowledge and understanding? Why doesn't God just tell us the answer? Well, besides the fact that we wouldn't believe Him, just as the land cannot yield its bounty to fallen man and man must now till or work the land to make it bring forth its fruit because of sin (Gen 3:17), we must study or work to gain the knowledge God wants us to have because we are no longer connected to the source of all knowledge (1 Cor 8:7). This is not to say that when we do this, we add anything to the sacrifice Jesus made, only that because of sin, we must choose to show the initiative that we desire to know more of what God has for us (Luke 11:24). Our fallen state no longer allows us to just receive of God. Knowledge must now be tilled just like the ground due to the entrance of sin.

You may ask, why knowledge and not some other aspect of life? What was the name of that tree our original parents, Adam and Eve, ate from? So, by knowledge, a thing which was meant for our good but used for our harm (Gen 50:20), God restores to us and uses knowledge for our good; by this method, God shows Himself the God above all gods (Ex 18:11, Psa. 108:5); above anything that presumes to hinder His plans. Have you ever thought of knowledge as a god?

This method of dethroning gods by our God is a standard He uses often (Ex 9:14); to use the very thing that is trying to bring us down, to lift us up higher; higher than we can even imagine. This is something only the real God can do. This makes Him indeed the God of gods, for (the eyes of the Lord go to and fro in the earth searching for those He may Himself strong) (1 Pet 3:12, 2 Chr 16:9).

This way of God also becomes a pattern that allows us to know what to look for in our relationship with God. It is how we can set our hearts and minds to anticipate what God has for us and to follow Him. It is the fuel for our faith. We are never without knowledge and knowledge is not necessarily truth. We must choose which knowledge we will believe. We must be aware that in most cases, understanding comes later. Do you think Adam or Eve understood what God or Satan was saying to them about their choice? No, they only needed to choose which knowledge to believe or whom to believe. The understanding, by living through the consequences, came later. Understanding is not necessary to be in or out of the will of God (Isa 1:19). In fact, to wait for understanding negates Faith, for the scriptures say we do not walk by our senses which feeds us knowledge about our surroundings (Heb 10:38). We are to be led by the Spirit (Rom 9:32). In those moments of confusion, when it is hard to tell what is right or wrong, we simply obey God (Isa 1:19). How do we obey? We obey by walking in the knowledge God has given us. Do you ever wonder why the Book? Why the Bible? Because it is The Knowledge. It is knowledge to counter the knowledge we, as a fallen race of beings, would now experience only through our senses because we are disconnected from the revelation knowledge of God, the true knowledge. This is what sin did; it separated us from knowing the truth (John 17:17).

The Bible contains a prism of the array of emotions and subsequent actions springing from the human experience. This information is there to help us through life. It gives us the chance to live the high life (Mat 7:14) and to know what's coming. In our current fallen state, the information in the Bible tells us where those emotions or actions (good or bad) will lead us and how to avoid certain outcomes. Since we can learn through knowledge without experiencing, The Book makes logical sense. We write letters, notes, or instructions to each other to influence behavior as a normal course of communication in our day to day lives. For example, haven't you ever texted a family member to stop at the store on the way home or to offer advice about a troubling situation? Why wouldn't God communicate like this too? Only His notes or instruction cover hundreds of years rather than the limited time we experience and involve the deeper meanings of life. There's nothing spooky about this if you really think about it this way.

But still, God is able to impart information to us in any manner, as the scriptures say, *"is anything too hard for the Lord?"* (Gen 18:14). Remember what I said about the narrative? The narrative is important. Let's say that you were watching a superhero movie and in the middle of the movie it changes to people in a cooking contest. Even if you like watching cooking contests, you would not expect this in the middle of the superhero movie. The first thing you would think is that someone taped over something or mixed up something. In other words, someone changed the narrative. You would be right because the two stories or narratives don't belong in the single context. You are either watching a superhero movie or you are watching a cooking contest but not at the same time. For those A type personalities out there thinking that you can have a cooking contest within a superhero movie or vice versa, yes you can but even then, the two stories would have a specific context to be acceptable.

So, we should think of the Bible like this. God has put in print the narrative He wants us to understand and follow. The Book must describe something of the narrative that God wants to share with us. Even His choice of how to get the information to us is descriptive of some idea that He is accentuating and once He sets the narrative, He will follow it out to the end (Isa 55:10-11). We are not allowed to add to it or take away from it (rev 22:18). Without understanding this, you won't be looking for it. So, you won't see the pattern. A very good example of this is the Jewish culture. In Jewish culture, pattern is prophecy, not necessarily the foretelling of an event, as in our culture. In their day-to-day living, Jews walk out the story of the Messiah in their holy days or the story of the bride in their marriage ceremony (Matt 25:1,6, Luke 5:35). If this is indeed a method of God, He will be consistent with it (Mal 3:6). I am taking time to point this out because I want this process or pattern to be a part of your thinking as I share what God has told me. Whatever we feel that God is working out in our lives, it must fit the narrative or story told in His Word. You will see that I'm not smart enough to see this on my own. Jesus had to explain this to me just as He will to you if you really want to know.

Let's start at the beginning of the story or narrative about the creation of our parents. The scripture says that God created man in His likeness (Gen 2:7) out of the dust of the ground. Do you think God wanted a child (Gen 1:26)? Notice that the initial creation of man represents a singular being. Man was put into the garden, God created, to tend it (Gen 2:15). Then God gave this singular being one line not to cross. God tells man to eat of any tree except from the tree of the knowledge of good and evil. God also gives the consequences of disobedience, death. Even at this point, with man being a singular being and connected to the revelation knowledge of God, do you think man fully understood what God was telling him? If you say no, then this acknowledges that man, being a creation, was only privy to certain information, which seems to be what Satan was suggesting to Eve. If you say yes, then this newly made man is suicidal because his eventual choice led to disobedience, which led to death. If you're saying, wait a minute Adam didn't sin first, he knew better but Eve wasn't there when God told Adam this so she had to be told later (by Adam) and she must not have believed him (I can't tell you how many times I've heard this) but then seduced Adam to eat; well, I submit that Eve was there in the beginning when God gave the commandment. She was in the loins of Adam as it were. In fact, there are some scriptures (Heb 7:10) that allude to the initial creation containing both male and female components in one body. This possibility is even found in nature. So, this is very plausible.

In every male human, there is a small part of female hormones and in every female, there is a small part of male hormones. Modern science tells us this. There are some species that contain both male and female components in one body and reproduce within themselves without a partner, bisexually. Why? I haven't found scriptures that specifically say this of man but why would there be examples in nature to make this idea very plausible? Why are there examples to attest to this possible state of being in our environment? Could it be that the things in nature are also a part of the narrative or story God is telling (Psa. 19:1)?

It is very possible that in the beginning of the creation of man, Adam had Eve's attributes contained in one body (Gen 2:22, the word 'rib' can also mean side, Strong's h6763) . Also, why would God create Eve out of Adam? Did He run out of material to make Eve? If He made Eve separately, would she not still be human or of Adam? Was God limited in some way (Gen 18:14, is anything too hard for the Lord)? What is God trying to tell us in the way he created woman?

At this point, I need to tell how this insight came into being and was revealed to me by Jesus. As I said, this happened many years ago. I was reading the Bible a lot back then, from Genesis to Revelation repeatedly. I didn't feel the need for any formal schooling because I knew Jesus was right there with me, teaching me. In my earlier years, I was very introverted, so I had a lot of time on my hands. I suppose I still have the personality of an introvert but God has pushed me out of myself to interact more with my others. Anyway, in those days, I was like the kid who asked all kinds of questions no matter how simplistic, like *"why is the sky is blue"* or *"why is water wet?"* While these types of questions can become annoying to our natural parents, God owns time, so He acted like He had nothing better to do other than to answer my childish questions. I had a lot of them.

Since I didn't spend a lot of time with other people, not even my family, I was always reading or in God's face about something. Well, one day I asked that question all children ask, *"where did I come from?"* However, since I'm talking to the Creator, I'm asking why do I look like this? Why do I have two arms rather than three? Why can't I fly like birds, etc.? You know what's coming, right? I got more answers than I could handle. Indeed, I couldn't handle the truth. I suppose this is why it never occurred to me, until now, to write about this or tell this story. I'm just beginning to accept the answers as a truth and to my surprise, more is given to those who have (Mat 13:12). The more we let God in, the more He tells us. God's answers to me are still strange to think about. It certainly changed the way I saw life then and has influenced me ever since.

Please understand, I don't expect you to

just believe me but I will give you scriptures to research so you can see where this is in the Bible or where these things are alluded to in the Bible. Again, I do expect you to study to show yourself approved (I Tim 2:5) and to simply ask Jesus yourself. Some things are too important in our belief structure to accept, based on the knowledge of others. I also have found that life is more bearable in the hard spots when you know that you know, you are exactly where God wants you to be, thinking exactly the way He wants you to think and doing exactly what He expects of you even if the situation is difficult or painful. The only way to know that you are doing this is to know Him and the best way to know Him is to read the notes He left you on the various subjects pertaining to your life in The Book, The Bible.

As I said before, to my knowledge, I have never heard anyone preach on what I'm about to tell you concerning Eve. Because of this, please, I implore you to confirm these things for yourself. Jesus said if we believe Him, we will believe each other because we will know the truth when we hear it (Luke 1;16, John 13:20, Mat 10:27). This must be so because the answers come from the same Spirit (Rom 5:5). Also, if this seems like new knowledge, why now? Well, God did say that some things are sealed up until the appointed time (Hab 2:3, Gal 4:2, 4). For Eve, I believe her time is now.

This is what Jesus answered me when I asked Him *"what are we and why do we look this way?"* He said that there are many things we are unaware of that occurred before we were created. Written in our creation is the story or narrative of some of those things. This is made evident by God so that even those in unbelief can see by nature God's handiwork (Rom 2:14, 1:18-23). In other words, as Shakespeare even said *"All the world is a stage and men and women are merely actors"* (As You Like It, Act II Scene VII) . Just as the God of Abraham, Isaac and Jacob wrote into the Law of Moses the motions of the redemption story or narrative, a higher view of man tells a story of things that occurred before man's creation. For example, the initial creation of man was in the existence of a singular body but another was with him and yet was him. Where have we heard this before? Well, let's look over at the gospel of John. It starts by saying *"in the beginning was the Word, and the Word was with God, and the Word was God"* (John 1:1). Can we say this of Eve? Could we say, in the beginning of man's creation was Adam, and Eve was with Adam, and Eve was Adam?

God told me that man's initial creation had two faces, a male and female face with one body that contained both functions. Does this remind you of the living creatures in Eze 1:5,6? In this state man was a bisexual being. As I said before, this idea is alluded to in nature. We see this also in the mythologies of other cultures. Just as other civilizations share the story of the flood which seem only like a mythos when one is not a believer of that particular culture; to one of that culture, it is a sacred belief. So, it is conceivable that in the bases of any mythology exist a truth.

Could it be that God at some point was a singular being that divided like the cells we see under a microscope to eventually become the Trinity we know now? From what God told me, this is what I get from the initial story of the creation of man. If our lives are indeed a blueprint to tell a story or narrative, then Eve's accepting of the forbidden fruit first rather than Adam and the way she was deceived, takes on a deeper meaning. Also, why didn't God divide Adam into a body of a trinity? A third being or sex. This would have fit the narrative of God the Father, God the Son, and God the Holy Spirit. God could have but He didn't. Or did He? I will leave you to explore these possibilities, in this manuscript, I merely want to plant the seed to help Eve grow to be who she was meant to be in this life and allow her to see Adam in a different light; closer to the way she must have thought of him before the fall. When this happens, they two will be one again (John 17:17) because they will know the truth. Unity is oneness and oneness is freedom. When they are one, we shall be one and we shall all be free. (John 8:32).

Oneness. How does God define this word? This word is the apex or crux of the issue that binds or separates Adam and Eve. The scriptures say that sin comes between God and man to break the connection or oneness God intended for us (Col 2:13). Remember that Jesus says that He is the vine and we are the branches (John 15:5). Without this connection, we can do nothing. If Jesus, Himself could do nothing without the Father, how can we expect to succeed in walking in the will or spirit of God without this connection? What more does Jesus say about oneness? In the gospel of John, He says a lot. In the whole of chapter 17, Jesus' prayer before his crucifixion to the Father, demonstrates

Their point of view on oneness (John 17:21). He was talking about his disciples but apply this to just Adam and Eve. How intense does this picture become? As He prayed for oneness, he often used the terms *"I in them, You in Me, they in Us"* (John 17:23). It is notable here to mention how God decided to allow man to procreate in their bodies by defining this act of oneness with the same action. Some of the words used by God to define our unity with Him contain surprisingly intimate or sexual imagery. When exploring this facet, it can well make one rethink our biological roles to understand that this action may be limited in our understanding as we define it or have been taught. In other words, from God's point of view, this act must have a higher meaning.

Alpha and Omega is the very definition of Jesus. He is the beginning and the end (Rev 1:8). What really does this mean? We humans, being bound by time can understand the beginning of something and the end of something but what does it mean for a thing or an entity to be both, in one instance of time? The beginning of something is always defined to us as a line in time where something starts. Since the start is no longer the same condition of the initial situation of whatever aspect we are talking about, we continue to draw a line to represent the change from the start. Then when the situation of whatever aspect we are talking about stops or ends, we stop drawing the line that represents the time it took to get to the end. The end is never the same as the start nor does the start ever touch the end for us. However, Jesus says He is the beginning and the end, the

Alpha and Omega. So, in Him the beginning and end touch. Jesus is not a line in time, if anything from our perspective, He is The Circle of time. He is The Oneness.

In our existence, there is never an instance in time where time doesn't matter or didn't occur. However, Jesus is the same forever (Mal 3:6). So, this beginning and ending can't be what we usually experience. It has to be something more but it can still be the same as the beginning or ending we experience from our perception. For the sake of making this concept simpler, let's just say this pertains to the beginning of the creation of man in the garden to the end state of man, the time we are coming upon. Where do we find ourselves now? In the beginning man was singular which could be nothing more than oneness. Man's own beginning and end. Even when Eve was created before they sinned there was still a 'oneness' yet a partitioning (Eph 2:14). Then through their choice that allowed sin to enter our existence, they truly became two separate beings. The connection they needed to be one was no longer there. They changed even more from the creation point and from the point in time of their physical separation. What's in the middle of the beginning and end? The story or narrative. The end of man is the story of them becoming one again. How do I know this? The scriptures say that Jesus is the same yesterday, today and forever, He changes not (Mal 3:6). What will this look like for us who have accepted his sacrifice? What will this look like for humans? Why do you think you know? However, if the beginning is the same as the end, then we can speculate what it will look like based on what we know of the beginning. It should look like the beginning again. It will look like Jesus.

B. THE FALL

When we read about the fall of our original parents into sin, sometimes the unsaid words speak louder than the words spoken. The unsaid words point to happenings with subtly that imply not only why God declared the new relationship Adam and Eve would now experience because of the introduction of sin in the world but also why God allowed the serpent in the garden in the first place. Later in other parts of the Bible such as in Isaiah and in Mathew, we find out even more details. In one example of this, in the garden when God tells man to subdue the earth (Gen 1:28), the unsaid words garner the questions of why man in an idyllic setting should need to subdue or take control of anything. This also implies that man is not the beginning of the story but being introduced into the story after it has already begun. If the scriptures indeed express that those in a higher plane relative to man's existence look in on the things of man to gain understanding (1 Pet 1:12), then the actions God takes to balance man until the Seed should appear would be instructional for those in that higher plane and a narrative pointing to the Seed so we and any other beings would be able to recognize Him when He appeared

(Gal 3:16). This would point to the higher narrative that began before man was created. This also means that our (man's) narrative, has not solely been written just for man. Here again we embrace Mosses' words that we live out our days as a tale told or rather in a specific narrative (Psa. 90:9) not of our choosing. This must be the main reason why we so often don't understand what is happening or being played out in our lives. We can't see the whole picture or we don't know the whole story. We may never know it in our lifetimes. Could this be why faith is so important in our relationship with God?

With this in mind, let's look at the dialogue of the fall of Man from a slightly different angle. Besides what will happen to man now under the curse, what specifically is being called out and why? What is specifically happening to Eve? Remember, God can do this any way he wants. Why this way? This angle that I'm about to discuss is very plausible especially when noting the outcome of the actions of man throughout the centuries in the structure of our societies based in the paradigm of a patriarchy, the acceptable actions recorded in the Law of Moses (Ex 23:17) along with Paul's writings (I Tim 2:12) and some of the responses of Jesus when He was asked about these things (John 1:17).

So, as we continue with the narrative: when God ask the man, in the garden, if he had eaten of the forbidden tree (Gen 3:11), his reply is to cast blame for his actions, you see that God doesn't address this at that point but moves to she which was blamed. Then God asked the woman the same question. She, like the man cast blame for her actions and again God moves to the one she blamed. God doesn't ask the serpent anything. Was the serpent's action a deliberate act based on understanding, therefore inexcusable with no explanation possible? God just pronounces the curse on it for its actions. God had already told the man that the soul that sins will die (Gen 2:17). So now the full meaning of their choice would be felt and seen through their senses. Now that man is separated from the revelation knowledge of God, man will have to gain knowledge only from their senses. Their natural reaction will be to hide from God (Gen 3:10). Their connection is severed and their ability to have the mind of God unreachable. In this state, "missing the mark" or sinning will be a natural inclination for them, for us. As this condition grows, the more their light dims and darkness takes over, the greater the separation will be. So now God must put up a partition between Himself and man while He works his redemption because darkness in the presence of God cannot exist (James 1:17, John 1:5).

It is worth noting that God defines Adam and Eve as Man. God did not name the wo-man Eve. Eve was named by the male-man. When God called Adam, they both came to Him. We need the further definition of our differences due to the separation and sin. So, when God says man, he includes both sexes. If God means something specific for the gender, He'll call it out so we'll know. This idea is similar to the word family. When someone says the word family, you don't think of all men or all women. You think of a compilation of people. Gender doesn't come into the picture. When I began to see this and understand why, I see the importance of this small concept to promote unity, God's unity for male and female. The enemy has us thinking that when something is referenced as 'for all men,' that this excludes women. This is not true according to the way God see it. So, we need to use language as God does to promote the unity God intends.

Now, let's go back to the specifics of the curse to unpack what will happen and what lies underneath what will happen. The serpent's natural form is cursed and in essence, its sense of being. Whatever it was supposed to be, it will not be that anymore. It is only destined to bruise the heel of the man. The only way this can happen is if the man is standing on its head. So, the serpent will eventually be subservient or overcome. We all understand that the body of the serpent was taken over by the adversary or our enemy; also named Satan or the devil (Rev 12:9). This curse then is directed to the adversary because he is behind the temptation of man. The serpent may have been beguiled into letting the devil speak through it, like Eve was. No matter how the devil got access to the serpent's body, it too is cursed. We are not given exact details about this however, the other stories in the Bible that relate demon possession of animals can give us a plausible clue how this could have happened. Also, did you ever wonder why God made man from the dirt? It is possible that before man was created during the turmoil in heaven (Luke 10:18), that God boasted to the fallen angels that he could make righteous, God-like beings from dirt that would be better than angels or now the devil?

It seems that whenever God makes a claim, the devil is there to try to counterman His words; to try and prove that God is somehow a liar. Could this be why Jesus highest name for the devil is the "father of lies" because He attaches to the devil the very label the devil tries to give God? This situation could be somewhat like the story in Job. Where God boasted of Job to the devil then Job's life became a story of perseverance and acknowledging God no matter the circumstances through the trials put to him by the adversary. This is exactly where we find ourselves because the actions and words of Job are what our faith in God demands of us even today.

Okay now, the specifics of the curse from Serpent then to Adam then to Eve will be described in this order because when I begin to discuss Eve, the rest of this book will be in respect to where Eve fits in the balance God created until the Seed should come through her and until the Seed reigns. Moreover, why God allowed things to develop like they have in man's history and what is God's redemptive work towards Eve as the narrative discloses. I suppose at this point I need to say that as the word is defined in our culture, I am NOT a feminist. I do not believe in the exaltation of Eve over Adam or that they are somehow equal which in our eyes mean the same, for several reasons. God told me some time ago that Eve will not make it without Adam and that Adam will not make it without Eve (I Cor 11:12). God also told me that He made them to be one and His word, which shows His intent, will not come back to Him void (Isa 55:11). Being one doesn't necessarily mean the same and not being a feminist doesn't mean I condone the maltreatment of Eve in the paradigm in which we live. Remember we are broken beings. Our movements, that seems natural, are not all condoned by God either. He rather has to endure them until the Seed makes all things right or righteous or in right standing with God. Also, have you ever thought about the ills that would be perpetrated on Adam if we lived in a matriarchy? Eve is broken too. If we lived in a matriarchy, I'm sure that some man would be at his desk writing a book titled *"Which Adam Are You."*

However, the most prominent reason why I don't believe in Eve's exaltation over Adam is that this attitude does not fit the narrative. In fact, God did not even give Adam headship over Eve! Surprised? About here you should be thinking of these scriptures that seem to say just that, "For the husband is the head of the wife, even as Christ is the head of the church..." Eph 5:23. Well, just keep reading.

"...And the Lord said unto the serpent, because

thou hast done this, thou art cursed above all cattle, and above every beast of the field: upon thy belly shalt thou go, and dust shalt thou eat all the days of thy life..." (Gen 3:14). So, God pronounces the consequences of Satan's actions. It is interesting to notice when God says *"because thou hast done this, cursed is..."* versus *"because thou hast done this, I will curse..."* Could this be a clue in understanding the difference between a reaction due to sin and what God had to alter because of sin? In His words, God would not be stating those things that had not changed due to the curse. In other words, it would make no sense for God to say, because of sin, now you will breathe air when Adam and Eve were breathing air before they sinned. Therefore, the things mentioned in the curse must represent a change from what formerly was. Also, if we can believe that God says what He means and means what He says then every word in the Bible is precise of necessity.

God has the power to create by saying, therefore, He must say exactly what he means otherwise, He will be in danger of breaking His own standard (even though this is impossible) which is what Satan is trying to prove to those who came before man, thru man; that God is a liar. God knew that Satan could not resist the temptation to draw his new creation from Him. As the others watched, if God had forbidden Satan to even talk to man, it would have appeared that God had something to fear from Satan; perhaps it could have even appeared to the angels that Satan was speaking a truth. Remember what happened to Job. God didn't stop Satan from testing him, He just gave Satan a line not to cross, and that is to say, Satan could not kill Job (Job 1:12). Also remember how Satan tempted Eve. The first words out of his mouth cast doubt, *"Did God really say..."* Can you see Satan saying this to the angles, *"Did God really say, His way is the only right way?"* God holds Himself to the same standard he expects of us. When He speaks a word or promise, He keeps it within the boundaries of the law he has given us. If one wants to have children with integrity, one must demonstrate integrity.

So, the curse of the serpent makes him cursed above any cattle and any animal in the field. This can also mean that although all animals are cursed too, the serpent is cursed even more than the others. God doesn't seem to mention anything about the life in water although we know that the whole creation groans because of sin (Rom 8:22). Could this be because He is only concerned with those things that will most likely interact with man on a regular basis? If this is so, could there be an existence that appears not to be touched, as much, by sin? In the flood of Noah, one would think that this wasn't an issue to the fish in the sea. So, were they exempted? I'm just asking these questions to stretch your thinking. This is how inspiration from God comes, through using the imagination he gave us.

Because of the curse, the form of the serpent is now changed. Even in its cursed state, snakes can show beauty in their skin coloring. We can only imagine how beautiful it looked moving in the upright position when it was not cursed. Another part of this curse is for the serpent to eat dust all the days of its life. Could this be a reminder that in the end, dirt will rule over it? There is never an end to dirt. It's everywhere. What do we know that was dust or dirt and shall return to dust or dirt? Man. This also might be the reason why God chose this as part of the curse and make the serpent (the Satan) slither in the dirt. When the end comes and the defeat of Satan is evident in real time, Satan will have had his fill of man or dirt.

"And I will put enmity between thee and the woman, and between thy seed and her seed; it shall bruise thy head, and thou shalt bruise his heel..." Gen 3:15. This part of the curse is most often taught as two consequences but it is not. At least this is how I have always heard it taught. I heard it spoken like the scripture says, *"I will put enmity between thy seed and her seed; it shall bruise thy head, and thou shalt bruise his heel."* This is not what the scripture says. There are three actions going on here, four if you consider the bruised heel a consequence of bruising the head. So, the three are: enmity between the woman and Satan, enmity between the woman's seed and Satan's seed, and it (the Seed of the woman) shall bruise thy head, and thou (seed of Satan) shalt bruise his heel. The curse doesn't give a separate outcome to the enmity between the woman and Satan. This is because the deliverance only comes from the

Seed; there is nothing the woman can do about the enmity. However, it also speaks to a particular stronghold among women fueled by the enmity between her and Satan. Which could mean that her particular spiritual warfare could have a caveat to it that is hardly preached about to give her deliverance in a more particular way. Mainly because this enmity is an *"I will"* statement from God, but more on this later when we come to the section on Eve.

"And unto Adam He said, because thou hast hearkened unto the voice of thy wife, and hast eaten of the tree, of which I commanded thee, saying, Thou shalt not eat of it; cursed is the ground for thy sake; in sorrow shalt thou eat of it all the days of thy life; thorns also and thistles shall it bring forth to thee; and thou shalt eat the herb of the field; in the sweat of thy face shalt thou eat bread, till thou return unto the ground; for out of it wast thou taken: for dust thou art, and unto dust shalt thou return" (Gen 3:17-19).

Wow! This is a mouth full. The whole history of mankind from the fall until now is contained in these verses, whereas God's response to Eve pertains solely to her job nested into the job her body contains. Perhaps this is why it is easy to believe that Adam had some kind of lordship over Eve before the fall. I've heard it preached that Adam was first so he has a greater responsibility over this life, over Eve. Well, this doesn't fit the narrative (John 1:1).

Could it be that God knew the best way to

balance man's life until the Seed should come? So, His pronouncement of the curse to Adam contains a hint of this plan. Think of it like this, if Adam had sinned first, could not God have said these same words to Eve? Why not? It seems to me that God was more concerned that Adam *"harkened to the voice of his wife"* instead of God's voice rather than who sinned first. How do I know this? Well, for one thing it would be mentioned in the scriptures if the order was important. Also, they were one and because they were one, they were equal but not the same. In our little minds, somehow equal means the same or deserving of the same treatment. In God's way of thinking, equal doesn't mean the same and this difference doesn't take away any responsibility or sanctity given by God. The most obvious example of this being the specific responsibilities Adam and Eve have because their bodies are different. You ever wonder why God didn't say to Eve when He pronounced her part of the curse, *"Because you harken to the voice of the serpent..."*? That would have been consistent with the order but the serpent is not equal to man (I Cor 6:3).

So now with sin in the picture, peace of mind would not be a constant state for man. As the old adage goes, *"idle hands are the devil's workshop,"* this could mean that man without something to occupy his mind, in this sin state, would be capable of destruction without a reason rather than basking in the contentment God had for him. This contentment would have not only produced life in him but also around him. Man would create because his maker is a creator. This part of the curse would seem to support this idea. Remember, God's main goal now is to balance life until the Seed comes; to keep man from destroying themselves until the Seed comes.

Now that man must till the ground for food and work for his needs, he will have little time to enjoy life as he would have before sin entered the world. Also, eating bread in sorrow speaks to food now not being able to rejuvenate him but only sustain him for as long as his body is able to function. It always amazes me how doctors, dietitians or nutritionist tell their patients to eat well to live healthy. We are not healthy; we are in terminal bodies. The best we can do is to eat well to die well (Mark 7:15, 18). I don't know about you but this makes me sorry as the scripture said it would.

The curse continues to say that man, on his best day, doing everything correctly, the ground will still produce rottenness or things he can't use for life, thorns and thistles. This part is where vegans get their oomph because they say God intended for us to eat vegetables, and the reason why they say humans are not supposed to eat meat. Well, I can't argue with them but if we don't eat meat, we still die so to your own conscious be true. Again, this state of being makes me sorry as God said it would.

Do you ever think about the things we have to do to survive? We all toil but in the wealthier nations we don't struggle so much day to day with these thoughts. However, put yourself in the shoes of those in nations where every day is a struggle to survive (Luke 6:21, Job 30:25). Afterall, we are all human beings and at some time, in some way, this will come to you (Luke 6:25). Notice that we have to do a lot to survive when you compare it to what God had intended for us. Before sin, essentially our food would have hung from trees. There would have been no preparing, no cooking, and no work behind getting it. Talk about true fast food! Nothing would spoil. Food would just be there for the taking and I believe we would not have had to eat every day. This is just something I believe because some of the scriptures talk about one meal that lasted a prophet for forty days (I Kings 19:8). Most of our time would have been spent learning of God, not toiling.

The lack of food can accelerate the cause of returning to the dust as well as having good food can decelerate this process of death. Since food can't stop death either way, we can understand more succinctly why Jesus said man will not live on bread alone but by every word from the mouth of God (Mat 4:4). I suspect since God's word can prevent death, the true food for life is the Word of God, therefore the food we consume is of a type to describe something in our narrative. But to have to eat it by the sweat of our brow (that sweat can also mean the wicked things we endure at work just to put food on the table), only to return to dust is most disheartening. Are you sorry yet? Are you anxious for the Seed to appear to save us from this? The promise of the Seed was what Adam and

Eve hung their faith on to continue. Remember, they had something to compare their new sin life to. They could remember what life was like before sin. We at least don't have those memories to haunt us but we do have the hope of the Seed.

C. THE FALL OF EVE

"Unto the woman He said, I will greatly multiply thy sorrow and thy conception; in sorrow thou shalt bring forth children; and thy desire shall be to thy husband, and he shall rule over thee." (Gen 3:16). Do you see the four things mentioned here? I can't call them all specific curses of God because some of these outcomes are the natural reaction of sin entering into the situation. The first thing mentioned is sorrow then increased conception then sorrow again but this word is slightly different from the first sorrow, fourthly an unfulfilling of her desire with a reaction specific to Adam's fallen state.

The definition of the first word 'sorrow' is the same word used to describe Adam's sorrow as he eats from the cursed ground (Strong's Con 6093). It means to feel pain or grievous toil. In a way, Adam's reproductive acts from the ground could be similar to Eve's reproduction in her body. Whatever produced would all eventually die. If we were to look at it this way, we can understand why God would use the same word here. However, from the next outcome mentioned, we can surmise that

28

Eve would not have reproduced so much before sinning because God said that He would 'greatly' multiply her conception. I can only speculate here from what we know about the result of sin entering the picture but man can now die so a broader base would be necessary to maintain their existence until the Seed comes. A broad base of mankind would make it harder for Satan to snuff out mankind. You know he would try because his intent is to dethrone God and His Word even through His creation. Increasing Eve's conception would be very helpful in this case.

Question, do you think this increase in conception meant that Eve would have more children in a shorter period or that Adam would have a stronger sex drive as she responds to him by producing more children to be born? This is just an interesting question I'm putting out there for you to ponder.

Well, the next declaration is that Eve will bring forth children in sorrow. This seems a little redundant if this word means the same as the first sorrow pronounced on her. This also implies that labor pains would have been unknown to Eve if sin had not entered. As I stated before, the sorrow in childbearing is not the exact same sorrow mentioned earlier (Strong's Con 6087 (idol)) . This sorrow has in it possible mental anguish whereas the first sorrow speaks to toiling or bodily fatigue. In other words, one's mind might be in anguish but it is not because the body is tired from toiling. The specific mental anguish could speak to the relationship Eve would have with the new life she is bringing into the world. After all she is the first person to get to know this new individual. With sin in the world, all the babe can do is cry to signify need. I believe before sin, Eve and Adam would know exactly what the babe is feeling or thinking even before it was born. This again would show a loss of a special connection God intended for all of us to experience. A special sorrow for Eve. This word "sorrow" also has the meaning of idol associated with it. This is very appropriate and interesting because it gets to the heart of why Eve's curse is different from Adam's but more on this later.

The last declaration from God to Eve is very interesting and holds several implications. Implication that, as I said before, I have never heard anyone preach. God said, "...thy desire shall be to thy husband, and he shall rule over thee..." When God separated Adam and Eve, it is logical to assume that he divided out whatever they were before the separation into two individuals. In other words, whatever God decided to give the male man, Adam, would be specific to his part in the story or narrative. These attributes would define this thinking or his job, so to speak. While they both would still retain some basic common attributes, the separation would allow particular attributes to be more dominate. Likewise, the female man, Eve, would experience the same condition.

The scriptures call Eve a helpmeet for Adam

(Gen 2:18). Why? Because he needed someone to rule over? Because she needed someone to tell what to do? What does the scripture say? The scripture says it was not good for him to be alone so Eve was pulled out of him to be a companion. To create a different synergy than he would experience as a singular unit in one body. So just as their body parts fit snuggly together in intimacy so also their minds should, to create a new type of unity. But sin entered in. Now Eve, designed to be the very essence of his desire, would desire only one thing she could not have, Adam.

What is desire? Webster's dictionary defines this word as a longing or craving. The hope of filling an emptiness towards completion. Yet in his fallen state, Adam would not be able to return the love Eve desires, which is more than physical. His concept of returning this desire would only be to rule over her or own her. The scripture could read, "...thy desire shall be to thy husband, BUT all he shall be able to do is rule over thee..." The use of the "and" in the scripture is used as a contrast word to point out the opposite of what was stated at the beginning of the sentence.

It would make no sense for God to state that Adam will love her to her desire since this is what they experienced before sin entered. Eve now is destined to live a life chasing the desire of Adam but he can only respond by possessing her. After nearly six thousand years of history playing out a story that describes this very state, this must seem natural to us. Thank God for His Truth! Thank God for Jesus! His sacrifice restores Eve to her rightful place to receive love as well as allowing Adam to bestow love; rather than leave her as unfulfilled chattel. This is a bold move by subtlety in the Book in the face of the patriarchy. Jesus must unveil this in this way because it is necessary to move in the truth of who Adam and Eve are for the total redemption.

A Curse before us? Have you ever seen that painting of a man painting a picture of a man painting a picture of a man? When one looks at it, there appears a reflection of the same scene getting smaller and smaller. What if our lives are like this? What if our lives tell a story that if we look back to the beginning, we see a reflection that can tell us a lot about who and why we are?

Do you remember what I said about the narrative or story? How it does not seem to have started with us. If God uses the same method to get information to us, as we have seen in scriptures; how a story is mapped out in a culture by the laws given to them by God, to walk out in their daily lives, a future state or prophecy then He must want us to know. He must want us to ask, why this way, why this story, why these facts? Remember, God can do this any way He wants. Nothing accidentally happens to Him. Because we experience accidents in our lives, thing we did not intend to happened, we tend to think this happens to God; like He doesn't know what will happen before it does or like He is waiting for things to unfold to decide what to do. No, God lives outside of time, we don't. Therefore, He can move around in time, our timelines, or lives, before we even live it to determine what He will allow.

Keep in mind that He made us for a reason. If it was simply to reproduce Himself, eventually as heirs, we would have to live in or deal with any conditions He is living in or dealing with, for instance, the concept of evil. This being said, could God be explaining to us the history of what occurred before we were created by the conditions of our lives; in our walking out our daily lives? In our narrative? Are we a picture of a picture of a picture? Reasoning like this can give us a clue as to why He let the serpent in the garden in the first place. To play out a scenario. It can also point to why the temptation was with the tree of life against the tree of knowledge of good and evil. Why isn't it the tree of life versus the tree of death? Although eating from the tree of knowledge produced death, why wasn't it called the tree of death? Is knowledge the same as death? I don't think so, this is another clue that something more is happening here.

Could God have said to Satan before our existence, curse is the universe for thy sake, decaying energy will it produce. Whatever you touch shall come to nothing. In darkness will you reside until light is restored. Words something like this. Because our concept of death is limited, all we can tell from death is that whatever Satan's punishment is, it is as abhorrent as we find death.

There are few, what I call, universal sins in

the world. These are sins that no one must teach you, yet you know how to do them, for instance, murder. Have you ever watched a child get really angry because a toy was taken from him or her? Have you ever seen how a child responds to its parent telling him or her that it is time for bed but the child doesn't want to go to bed? Do you think in that moment of time if the child could overpower the person or parent, that the child would be able to kill? Well, this is what happened to Cain. Think about it. Cain had no example of killing, except for the animals for clothing or in offerings yet he made the leap to kill his brother. Granted that he was probably experiencing emotions that he had never experienced before and had no other human that could have understood his feelings because he was the first one to go this far. So, his rage played out to what is common place for us today.

Let me offer you another plausible scenario that could have contributed to his disposition. The promise God made to Eve that her seed would save them was ever present in Adam and Eve because I'm sure they want to go back to the garden. Do you suppose Eve told Cain that he was the One? If so, then Cain would think that any offering he made would be alright with God. Oh, by the way, the scriptures allude to God accepting the offering by sending fire to consume it. So, when Abel's offering was consumed and Cain's was not, of course he was angry because after all he was the One to save the world. Adding rage to rage in this situation by Abel telling Cain what was right; I bet

Cain never missed a chance to tell Abel that he was better because he was going to restore them back to God. Remember the Pharisees interaction with Jesus? The scriptures say they were jealous of Him. Could this have been the first time Cain let his pride make him fail before God? To be rejected by God was something he thought could never happen because he was the savior?

Anyway, we tend to spiritualize the things we read in the Bible but if we except that the people in the stories are just as fallen as we are, things sometimes make a little more sense when we are reading. So, Cain kills his brother and everyone realizes that he is not the one. We can tell this by Eve's statement when she has another child. She says that Seth is appointed as another (Gen 4:25). You think she was still believing? I know so. I would imagine that Adam and Eve were a little surprised, like Paul when they approached their deaths and the appointed one (or time) did not appear. God reserves times and seasons to Himself, as Jesus said, (Act 1:7) and in our fallen state, it seems to put us in a depressed or negative place when we think of God working out a situation over hundreds or thousands of years rather than in the now.

With this in mind, what attitude do you think developed towards Eve as man or humans waited on the Lord for the savior? Probably not what you have been taught. The Bible begins the story of civilizations with Nimrod, as men began to move over the face of the earth (Gen 10:8). However, there are small remnants of stories that point to a possible matriarchal society that formed initially. You'll have to do your own research into this to come to your own conclusions about this. However, when one thinks of the human psyche, in this broken state, the idea of a matriarchy is very plausible. Although no one is recorded as dead except Able, at this time, everyone saw how terrible that was. I bet everyone gained a better understanding of why the savior was needed. The human mind would become more anticipatory and need some way to express this. So, naturally uplifting the one who would bring the savior, Eve, would be the next best thing to do until the savior comes.

This is not what God wanted, the reason being seated in why Eve fell. So, God Himself, establishes the patriarchy. How do I know that God established the patriarchy? Think about it. We as humans, cannot agree on anything especially across nations or ethnicities yet we established a basis for civilization throughout history that was uniformed in one way; in that, men, the male man, was in charge and the woman, the female man, was not. This created a sort of balance, until the Seed should come. It kept under control the fundamental imbalance in men and women. For a man, based on the way sin is said to have entered into the world in Genesis, he needed a pull towards action because he just stood there and let this happen then he was led by Eve; for the woman, she needed a pull towards inaction or an action monitored because she took the initiative without considering Adam then started giving commands, like God. When you look at the motions caused by the patriarchy, men are forced into actions to further the civilization and women are forced in to a submissive role; a passive role designed to inhibit her participation. Men being the head of the household or over Eve is the result of the curse (I Cor 11:3). It is not an exultation. Remember, this is the result of sin, it is not what God intended.

Now, on the surface, this appears to be a punishment by God because he is mad at Eve but when we grow up and understand that Gods ways are higher than ours (Isa 55:9) which makes his responses more for our benefit rather than a knee-jerk reaction to what we have done in His face, we begin to understand that there must be a higher reason for what He allows.

If you look at Eve's response to the temptation, she simulated the response of another being that wanted to usurp the throne of God. Remember the five "I will" spoken by Lucifer in Isaiah (14:13, 14)? We could rephrase these statements to say, I think, I will ascend; I think, I will exalt; I think I will sit; I think, I will ascend above; I think, I will be like God. So, in Genesis 3:6, where we are given an insight into what Eve was thinking, this scripture could be rephrased to show her five "I will" attitudes. The first I will – I think it is good for food (God didn't tell her this); Second, I will – I think it is pretty to look at. The third and fourth 'I wills' have to be inferred because they are logical conclusions to this line of thinking. The third I will – I think it smells good; the fourth I will – I think it taste good; the fifth I will – I think I will eat it to become like God. The point I'm trying to make is that Eve went through a thought process independent of what God told her. She decided that what she wanted was more important than what God told her. For the first time, in her life, she became aware that she could have an opinion apart from what God said. She became self-aware.

Based on God's reaction when Satan did this, God had to shut down Eve or she would have destroyed all of humanity. Actually, she did but God had a contingency plan for this choice. God had to introduce a system that would keep her subdued until the Seed should come.

The other universal sin I want to talk about, because the patriarchy fits so well into the mindset of the male man, the reflexes of the paradigm cause a type of second-class status of women even among the more progressive countries. No matter how many laws are enacted or how much education is promoted, this way of being will never go away until Jesus comes back. We only have the two choices: to walk in the flesh (the kingdom of man - patriarchy) or in the spirit (the kingdom of God while we experience the patriarchy and wait upon the Lord).

CHAPTER II

COME BACK UP HERE: REPENT

A. THE MOVE FROM ALPHA TO OMEGA

So now as we move through the progression of time, we move from our beginning or Alpha thru our progression in time or towards the end of God's plan or the Omega. Remember God is outside of time so from His point of view He just always is in the now, even when he visits our past and future. However, from our point of view, we become aware of the history that is behind us and realize that there will be history in front of us that will eventually be behind us while we are in the now.

The word pent means that something is placed or confined in a particular position or way of being . To put the prefix 're' in front of pent can be thought of as saying, return this to its original position or time; to come back up here where you were (originally) or in the past. In our modern vernacular, we define repent as changing one's mind to agree with God. So, when Jesus says in

Mathew 3:2, "repent for the kingdom of God is at hand", this can be translated as "change your mind and come back up here where you were initially, think like God again". However, as children governed by time, it will take us time to get back to the beginning again. God knew this, thus his plan and narrative that He has been working before our beginning till now (John 5:17, Heb 4:3). Not only will we grow in understanding and wisdom, our experiences will allow other to grow too (I Pet 1:12). This is the ultimate reason for this narrative of our lives.

What do you think happened after Adam and Eve were evicted out of the garden? What does the Bible say? First of all, it doesn't say they were removed as a punishment. It says that they were removed so no lasting harm could be on them; so, they would not have the chance to eat of the tree of life and remain in their fallen state forever. Anyway, chapter four of Genesis says they begin to conceived children. Eve's statement in verse one shows that she was excited about having a man child. You think she was hoping beyond hope that her boy was the one to restore them to the garden? As I said earlier, I believe so. I know so, but things didn't turn out this way. This child turned out to be the first murder among men. When we look in verse 25 of Genesis, Eve is again displaying her hope of the seed, for she says, "God had appointed me another seed instead of Able". If we can get a hint of the anticipation of the Seed in Eve's words, what do you think this anticipation looked like from Adam's point of view? Do you think Adam or the male man would revere Eve, the female man, because God made the promise to her and he too is hoping beyond hope that they can return to Eden?

When I was in college (in the 1990s), I took a religious studies class and I had a male professor that seem to be a feminist. He took the religions of the world and expounded the basis of their beliefs while demonstrating the severe, unfair patriarchal slant of the behaviors in such a way, every woman in that class left it mad. He seemed to delight in doing this especially with the Christian religion. One of the interesting pieces of proof he used was a book that must be out of print because I had searched for it for a long while and was unable to find it nor was I able to find most of the determinations in the book on the internet as just information. It was almost as though this information had been expunged. This may not be the case; it may be that the information is so old that it seems out of date and just hard to find. When I gave up on finding this book, I have since forgotten most of the particulars of this book because our sense of self should come from what God says, not from what man says.

Since I have some degree of respect for knowledge, I'm ashamed to admit that at the end of that class, I threw that book away because the author's assertions got to me too. In all the time I was in school, even grade school, I can't remember a time when I threw a book away. However, there is enough information in various places to backup or make the arguments this professor gave, in that class, seem very plausible. Although, we will only hold to the examples that support the information from my professor, that are alluded to in the Bible;

let's look at the main ideas from various sources anyway.

It is plausible to believe that the beginning of civilizations would be matriarchal because Adam and Eve were hanging on every word God gave them and for God to say that Eve would have a child that would restore their relationship, would affect their way of thinking so much that they would make assumptions about situations not necessarily based on what God told them. After all, now their understanding is limited because they are no longer connected to God and their view of life is distorted due to sin. Just extrapolating from the psychology of humans, can you accept that Eve could have possibly been proud of herself because she would give birth to the one to restore mankind to the garden and Adam would extol her as something to be worshiped because of this?

Although this is partly supposition, I believe that this is a part of our history that is missing. This is what was promoted in that book from my college class, that the beginning of civilization was based on a matriarchy. However, as time progressed and God begin to move on his time schedule and the Seed didn't appear when expected by man, Adam begin to believe in himself with help from the Adversary and to adopted a mindset of might makes right. When this happened, Eve would not be able to contend with this way of being since Adam was physically stronger than her and he held her desire. Thus began the patriarchy. A paradigm under which God works out his plan.

Springing from one of the exertions of my

professor, that I could not forget, was the origin of a word we still use now in a derogatory way as it was intended; it still lives in me as a scar. This word is 'motherfucker.' According to my professor, this word has its origin in the transition from matriarchal governance to patriarchal governance; where in a matriarchy the mother or woman was akin to the head of the family, like a mystic or shaman. This act of dominance speaks for itself in the word. The male mindset, to usurp female dominance is through the violence of physical strength or overpowering. Physical strength is the male attribute. The act of rape is not only an assault on women but also on the sacred promise given to her by God. As this act is carried out, the strongest man, the bravest man would rape his mother in the open, in the presence of the community, to show his dominance. This would subjugate the women because she is not strong enough to withstand him and this act would fill the men with dread to challenge such a revered personage. Rape is an act of dominance and theft but never love.

The book my professor used in that class noted that in the time of the matriarchy, women were seen as mystical. So, there was a mystical type of respect for women in general due to act of childbirth. This respect would be similar to what is afforded to a holy one or relic. The control comes from what one believes. To debase any woman would be the beginning of male men realizing their own self-awareness and begin promoting aspects particular to the male man.

So, a proof that backs up this historical

possibility is the etymology of the word 'shaman.' It is very fascinating if you are interested in researching this for yourself. Also, just in case you think all this is far-fetched or that we are too evolved to think like this, I encourage you to read 2 Samuel 16:21.

Let's define the patriarchy to be sure we are all thinking the same way. Not necessarily agreeing with the definition but at least we are coming from the same point of view. The Webster Dictionary defines patriarchy as: social organization marked by the supremacy of the father in the clan or family, the legal dependence of wives and children and the reckoning of descent and inheritance in the male line; (Broadly: controlled by men of a disproportionately large share of power). If this doesn't explain the last six thousand years, I don't know what does. The main question Eve should have, if she understands that God loves her too and is not mad at her, is why He has allowed this? Well, we'll get to this as I continue to develop the narrative God is working out.

As I stated before, the fact that the patriarchy is the basis of world governments and no nation can agree on anything else, must be a God inspired situation. If God felt so strongly that this paradigm is need as a basis to get from one state of being to another, or more succinctly, to further His plan or narrative, the question to ask, unbiasedly, is why? If you assume that God is good and cares for both states of man (male and female) then this paradigm would have to fulfill two basic principles, given the situation with sin in the mix, to succeed; the first one being that this paradigm is necessary for men but doesn't irrevocably harm them and the second being that this paradigm is necessary for women but doesn't irrevocably harm them.

Now I know you have to be thinking about the horror stories of male dominance that happens now and throughout history to women and wondering how this can be a good thing. Well, I ask you how much of that is the sin in the male man versus the sin of the paradigm? For example, when we think of the first murder, did this occur because of the paradigm of the sacrifice or was it because Cain was jealous of Able? As humans we want to say this murder wouldn't have happened if God had just accepted both of their sacrifices. However, this is not how it works. Remember we are approaching God to repent or going back up to where He is and He is a holy God. You just can't approach God any way you want especially with this sin in us. From our point of view, a lot of things make sense to us and are 'good enough' but from God's point of view, a lot of things we do are insanity and filthy (Isa 64:6).

So how could this paradigm be necessary for the male Adam? A clue is to look at how he broke when sin entered. What characteristics became perverted and what characteristics became subdued that needed to be in the forefront when making decisions or just in daily life? In other words, how different is he now versus how he was before sin entered? There are clues of this all throughout the bible. There are clues of this in the way God structures the law given to His people. One example that springs to my mind is from

Paul's writing in Ephesian's chapter 5:6, where Paul says, "...every one of you in particular so love his wife even as himself; and the wife see that she reverence her husband." So, this is a clue as to where the sin lines are drawn in men and women; without sin in them, God wouldn't have to say this. Why does Paul say to the men to love their wives? Because this is a point of 'pressing into God' that is necessary for men. Without the spirit of God in them, men do not by reflex love their wives. Men can equate sex with love or ownership with love but this is not even the beginning of love. These can be rather an expression that stems from all the things that make up love. We can also see from Genesis 3:16, as I stated previously, that Adam in his sin state would only be able to rule over Eve. Jesus only both rules over us and loves us. Praise be to God for this!

So, the unregenerated man (which is all men until the Holy Spirit became available) would equate rule or dominance with love and the natural flow from this way of thinking would display itself as needing control over any situation and this is the definition of the patriarchy. This reflex of needing control is heightened where women are involved. This is why the patriarchy is necessary for men and doesn't hurt them. It fits snuggly into their sin thinking. I have observed men and governments, stymie without this control, even only among men, with no women involved but once control is defined all arguments end (which doesn't mean that the fighting ends). This has been the cycle since the fall, it just repeats itself. Something like in the animal kingdom, the strongest wins until another that is stronger comes. This was necessary until the Seed should come. The patriarchy afforded God the time needed until the Seed should appear.

So how could this paradigm be necessary for the female Adam? Well, Eve was the first to become self-aware. Since they were moving away from God, this is not a good thing. However, this means that she would be slightly ahead of the male Adam in defining self but they were supposed to grow together as one. Because of the course they were now on, it would become necessary for her to wait on him to become one again. She would need to be slowed down or be subdued just as the other usurper (Isa 14:12-15). This is what the patriarchy does. What actually happens throughout time is that the male Adam becomes self-aware. He must trek in the wrong direction, away from God to meet her then to move forward with her. This was his sacrifice to her. This time of moving forward with her, I believe is now. It may seem like women are advancing themselves to become equal with men but this is not what's happening. Women will take their rightful place beside men in God's kingdom of kings and priests with the responsibility that God has designated for them, not for the male Adam.

In Ephesian's 5:6, why didn't Paul say to the wife, 'see that you love your husband?' Because she already loves him! She just doesn't respect him! This is Eve's failing as sin broke her. There is something in Eve that doesn't need to be in charge to get what she wants. I can think of several couples, in a struggle for control and the woman will let him think or be whatever he wants as long as she gets what she wants in the end. Eve is not stymied at the point of submissiveness yet subdued; still on occasion, she can go too far in wanting her desires fulfilled by demanding what only God should have. After all, her first want was to usurp God. This is why the patriarchy is necessary for female men and doesn't hurt them. The patriarchy affords God the time needed until the Seed should appear and the way is open to come back up here towards God or to repent.

A matriarchy is a move away from God because it challenges God's authority. Eve has the ability to get into Adam in such a way that it can be a challenge to the sovereignty of God. This is the exact point where she and Adam fell into sin. Eve took of the forbidden fruit because she wanted to be like God but Adam took of the forbidden fruit because he allowed Eve to become his God. Remember that God calls out Adam because he 'harkened to the voice of his wife,' (Gen 3:17) God didn't say this to Eve about the serpent when she listened to it and ate of the forbidden fruit. It must be that what happened between Eve and the serpent was sensual. The conclusion Eve came to by listening to the serpent was a process that involved her choice alone. She was not giving control to another as Adam did. Could this have been how she was deceived? In other words, she was deciding to be her own god, like she had a choice. According to the scriptures, Adam was not deceived. He knew better but still chose Eve to obey rather than God.

Can you imagine what a matriarchy would do

to Adam? God would be contending with Eve for his attention in an area where only God belongs. What does God say about sharing his authority (Ex 34:14)? They were designed to support each other in a very intimate way. Now that sin has entered the picture, this way would be perverted. Adam will want to own her and Eve will want to possess him. One can almost say, Adam wants to own her outside and Eve wants to own his inside. This again demonstrates the lines of declination in them that can define how sin broke them. It is also a clue to what they were before sin entered in.

It should be obvious that one can control a person's outside without owning their inside or their soul. A good example of this would be slavery. The core of every revolt in any form of slavery is that the inner man wants to be free along with the outer man. However, if someone or something owns the inner man or the soul, this person or thing possess the whole man. Again, God gets a bit testy when someone tries to step into his shoes. So, a matriarchy would promote Eve's sin mind and destroy Adam's ability to see the true God.

Adam is already in Eve's inner self where only God belongs but in his sin state, he is unable to take advantage of this because he is only able to respond by ownership. He is not able to fill her desire, thus she is always, in a sense, chasing him for true love. Even in her unregenerated state, Eve has a higher sense of what this love is. This is to her misery. As she goes about to control Adam's inner self, she becomes more and more disillusioned. She learns that being God is not as attractive as it appeared. This leads to her disrespect of Adam, thus Paul's assertion. This has been Eve's lesson to learn throughout history as this narrative unfolds.

B. THE MATRIARCHY IN THE BOUNDS OF THE PATRIARCHY

If we look at recorded history of the interaction between men and women, we will see definite patterns of behavior that seem to define the male and female way of thinking, when it comes to gaining control. We could go on and on with examples but let's just look at one or two so we are sure we are all thinking along the same line. Looking, especially, at the heads of governments or civilizations, we can see this pattern more vividly in the struggle for dominance.

Men work the obvious dominate scenes that involve acts of war and government rule by laws, while the women insinuate their will into the situation by more subtle ways. This correlates with the obvious rationale of men being physically stronger so force is a reflex; while women, as Peter puts it, are in the "weaker vessel" so mental ingenuity is a necessity (I Pet 3:7). One of the most well documented stories, of the ancient Roman empire, that portray the different way men versus women exert dominance is the story of Agrippina . She was the mother of Emperor Nero. Claudius was father to Nero and Agrippina's husband. She conspired with Locusta, a woman considered a professional poisoner and sorceress, to kill Claudius so Nero would become emperor sooner rather than later. If this had been a male adversary, a more direct way of assassination would have been attempted. However, Agrippina did tread where no woman had before in the Roman Empire but she still had to do this by manipulating men.

Nero, following his mother's lead, employed Locusta throughout his reign to poison his enemies. This is a clue that Nero's mother had more control over the throne than Nero himself. When the men of the Roman Senate grew tired of Nero's antics, they conspired to assassinate him but Nero kill himself before they could carry out their plan. The men weren't looking to poison him or contrive some scheme, they were simply going to kill him outright. When Locusta was no longer protected by Nero, the story is that she was executed. However, there was a more colorful story of her demise. She was supposed to have been raped to death by a specially trained animal and then torn to pieces . Whether this is true or not, the emphasis is on the worse atrocity that can be done to a woman and by an animal no less.

A biblical story of this kind would have some variations on it as the people would be taught of God not to do certain things but their humanity would still exert itself due to the sin nature. The subtlety of this story springs from the same root though; the story I mean is in I Kings 16, when Jezebel instructed her husband, King Ahab, on what to do to possess another man vineyard that he had no right to possess. She uses the king's seal to write falsehoods to get the man killed on the word of his false accusers so her husband can take possession of the vineyard. Here again, if Ahab had dealt with this situation as the man rather than letting his wife take care of it, he would have chosen a more straight-forward way to get the property. The point I'm trying to make is that to the male mind, direct confrontation is the norm and subtly for control is a woman's way.

I do know that we are approaching a time where the norm is hardly like what we have experienced in the recent past but I expect to stay within the initial intention that God described in the Bible then progress towards the deviations of our time, due to sin. We all know that we have the knowledge to make humans intentionally or inadvertently with extra limbs or missing limbs. If over the centuries the norm became people with extra limbs and those with only two arms and legs became the minority, would this take anything away from the original form of Adam and Eve? I think I saw a Twilight Zone episode that asked this question once.

What manner did God choose to maintain mankind until the Seed should come? God had to keep them away from his holiness so mankind wouldn't die immediately yet interact with mankind to unfurl his plan and save mankind. This plan He devised we usually call the Law. The Law allowed man to live in his terminal state and still approach God. The Law slowed down the death process until the Seed should come.

What is interesting about this plan is how it interacts with Eve. One would think that both Adams approaching God from a sin state would require the same steps. The differences are most telling. Let's explore some of them and see what they mean for Eve.

First, we can start off with the law requiring only that the men present themselves and serve in the Temple (Ex 23:17). The women seem to be excluded from this. Without explanation, it would seem that in spiritual things, Eve is only required to do what is expected of a woman, to tend to her husband, children and the home. God will overlook her sins as her husband obeys the law. There are a number of explanations for this that is even true today. The main reason being that lust would interfere with the worship due to the lack of self-control in our sin state. This is displayed in the pagan cultures of the time that allowed women in their temples. The temples basically became whore houses.

Continuing, we can look at an overview of the sacrifices God required under the law to deal with or 'cover' sin actions of the people so they could approach his Holiness until the Seed could come to take away sin with His true sacrifice. To begin, we will look in the book of Leviticus (chapters 1-8), which describes the sacrifices that point to Christ; the Burnt offering-this sacrifice was a male animal and is totally burnt up on the alter to appease God, the Grain Offering-this offering is flour and incense made to be a sweet-smelling savour before God, the Drink Offering-this offering is mentioned in Numbers 15 and wine is poured onto the alter sometimes along with the other offerings; this speaks of commitment. Remember what Christ said about drinking his blood when He gave them the wine (Mat 26:27, 28)? The Peace Offering-this sacrifice can be a male or female animal merely to approach God in thanksgiving; the Sin Offering-this sacrifice was a male animal made to cover guilt for a known sin and lastly the Trespass Offering-this sacrifice was a male animal and included compensation for an infraction.

All these offerings were to be offered without a blemish in the animal and represent an aspect of Christ's sacrifice. These offerings also speak to our guilt consciousness as we learn, through the law, what sin is. The offerer believed God, through the offering, that he or she was back in right-standing with God when the sacrifices are offered.

God devised this method in the Law to help us understand His feelings when dealing with sin and how horrible sin and death should seem to us. We also learn that now we cannot approach his holiness without a sacrifice. These sacrifices had to have been instituted at the time of Cain and Able for Able to know what the acceptable sacrifice was.

Do you remember why Paul said the Law was instituted? It was not made to make anyone holy; the law was made to expose sin and make sin seem more sinful (Rom 3:20, 5:20, 7, 8:2). Also, through the law, we embrace certain ideas that become a part of the paradigm that we live in. As I said before, the balance God puts in place until the Seed should come will help Adam and Eve to sustain their existence. There is no way to correct this problem of sin until the Seed appears so the law is merely a means to an end.

What I want to show from the working of the law and sacrifices is that the male animal sacrifices were specific to particular sins. These particular actions necessary to carry out the sacrifices gave birth to ideas that fit into our sin thinking, especially to a male mind for whom the paradigm we live in is derived. Not that God condoned these ideas but God knows that we grow from any point we find ourselves towards the truth. So, most often He meets us where we are with patience. God often uses a point of ultimate sin, to us, to show his strength over it; demonstrating that He alone is God over all things. Is anything too hard for the Lord (Gen 18:14)? We can learn a thing or two about dealing with difficult situations by acceptance and faith from God. Occasionally, God also allows our assumptions to seem acceptable by God to keep the enemy guessing. When He reveals the truth, it is freeing for all except the enemy.

So, the offerings that call out male versus female animals or a difference in an acceptable sacrifice depending on whether the offerer is a male or female and the amount of time or compensation required, tells us a little more about how Eve will be perceived in the law and situations. These differences offer our broken minds subliminal suggestions. Do you think God is wrong in letting us think we are right when we are wrong? Well, in God's defense, He tell us we can always ask and He will tell us. Our problem is that we don't ask because we arrogantly think we know. This, incidentally, is the exact basis of the sin of taking of the Tree of the Knowledge of Good and Evil.

Anyway, if we look at the female sacrifices, what's required is different and one could reasonably imply to a sinful mind that the female is worth less or requires more because she is more sinful. For example, the time of purification is twice as long for female childbirth than for a male child born and could imply that females are more sinful because they require more time for purification (Lev 4:28, 27:1-8, Lev 12).

This is not what God thinks but the law, given by God, is written in such a way to imply this and with subtle ways to show that Eve is needed. God even used this subtly to surprise the enemy into defeat. As Eve begins to understand what God is doing now, we must not repeat the original mistake but submit to the will of God and acknowledge that God only is God.

Let me give you another crude illustration of this phenomenon. God equates darkness to evil. Examples of this are just about everywhere in the Bible (Gen 1:2, 15:12, Prov 4:19, Jude 1:6). This idea led the early church to equate darkness to blackness which in turn made the early church equate blackness to evil. If you know our history, not just American history, you know the outcome of this way of thinking. The conclusion was that every human being not white or light skinned was evil. This can be proven by the early writings of the church and information (taken as truth) that was later removed from the sub-text of Bibles from the nineties and earlier. I remember watching Pastor Frederic Price preach on this in the nineties. I invite you to look up his research to be startled. I believe you can find some of his teaching under the title, "Race, Religion and Racism" on YouTube.

These are very good examples of how the paradigm we live in, that God put in place, reinforces certain ideologies to hold us to a certain way of thinking. Remember God is making the best of a bad situation. As we grow in His spirit to understand that these things are outgrowths of sin and while we obey, we are not bound by them. This is called 'growing up in the Spirit' (Eph 4:14, 15). This is also why God could say through Paul that "all things are lawful to me" (I Cor 6:12) and we are free from the curse of the law, Christ being made a curse for us (Gal 3:13).

The part that puzzles us is that we have to remain in this paradigm until Christ returns. Even in our day to day lives, not everyone has been or is in the 5th grade or not everyone has graduated from school. So, even though you might not need 5th grade teaching, there will be others behind you that will need this teaching. So, the process or structure for instilling the 5th grade lesson is still necessary. This is one reason why we continue to obey the constrains of the law and patriarchy until Christ comes. The other reason is that we still dwell in these sinful bodies that are prone to relapse, so there are times where we need this structure. Even Paul said while knowing Christ, he still did those things not allowed by the Spirit unwillingly (Rom 7:15, 16).

Therefore, we must submit to this paradigm or environment as long as we are in this environment until the Seed should appear, for the second time. This is why Christ said he did not come to destroy (the law) but to fulfill (Mat 5:17). As we grow in our walk in the Spirit, we wait like Joshua and Caleb for the others to be ready to join us and for the time when God is on the move (Num 14:30). This is what the last two thousand years have been about. While we are waiting on the Lord, there are still parts of His plan that have not occurred because it is all in His timing.

If this is understood, while we wait on the Lord patiently and with onerous anticipation, submitting should be just as burdensome to a man as it is to a woman, if one understands that the unity of the spirit is what makes us whole or one and this oneness makes us free (John 8:36).

I have just given a glimpse into the offerings, that every Christian should know in order to understand what Christ has done for us. I encourage you to do a study of this on your own. The most comprehensive study of the whole Bible I have seen was accomplished by Chuck Missler of Koinonia House. Although Mr. Missler has gone to be with the Lord, these teachings can be purchased and some can be viewed on YouTube.

As I said before, the outgrowth of the law, inspired the rudiments of the patriarchy which gave way to certain ways of thinking. This is true not just for men but for women too. Remember the law was designed to strengthen Adam's hands while subduing Eve's. For instance, men were allowed to own possessions such as lands animals and people because in his broken state, all Adam can do to relate is to "rule over" things (Gen 3:16). The woman only had these possessions through marriage. A man was able to have many wives. A woman was never able to have more than one husband at a time. Remember, these are consequences of sin, not necessarily the way God wanted things to be.

However, these outcomes are not written in stone neither are they always detrimental to women. When things are done in love, there are many ways we can move towards truth but there is only one door. I'm reminded of an incident that was recorded by Christian missionaries that went into a part of the world, I believe in the 1700s, that had not been explored. When the missionaries came, they found a small thriving society ruled by women that had many husbands. For that matter, the husbands also had other wives but there was only one alpha female that was over all the husbands and wives. These alpha females owned everything that could be possessed and made the laws. It is needless to say what happened, the missionaries explained to the men how they were the ones God put in charge and that society was destroyed.

Anyway, what does the law look like from Eve's point of view? Remember, her desire is for him (Gen 3:16). So, to have to settle to be one of many wives has to be less fulfilling than even to be wife of one husband that can't respond to you except to acknowledge that he owns you. When we look at this as it is described in God's narrative, having more than on wife has its place. After all, Jehovah, Himself, has two wives, Israel and the Church. It may be that this impulse has its place in the beginning to populate mankind and that man was not able to be, as Paul put it "husband to one wife' (I Tim 3:2), until after the Holy Spirit became available.

There is another process that we don't usually think of as the law or religious law, this is nature.

We think of natural laws but we don't think that nature was altered to assist the law God put in place for societies after sin was introduced. Let me give you an example. In Galatians, Paul talks about the Seed coming under the law, in other words made by a woman, to do the work of God in the earth (Gal 4:4). This means that God will limit certain actions dealing with mankind to what happens in the natural to mankind. Here again, is a subtlety that points to a particular struggle that could only belong to Eve. This is the enmity between the serpent and the woman (Gen 3:15). Although there is enmity between the serpent and the whole of mankind, there still is a special enmity called out between the serpent and the woman that excludes the male.

This gives more than one meaning to I Tim 2:14-15. I've heard this preached as if women must continue to give birth, however, I believe this scripture referred to the Seed that should come. The emphasis is on the Seed that should come not the childbearing. This has to be why, Jesus never said after He came, to pray to my mother then she will ask me to grant your prayer. He couldn't say this because it would promote the very reason that Eve sinned. She was attempting to usurp God's authority. It should also be noted that even in her sinful state, Eve is amazingly creative, cunning and dangerous. So, what is the path for her, back to their original state with God? The law (or patriarchy) until the Seed comes.

Ever wonder when Jesus was alone with a woman or women what he talked about to them? Why do we always assume that what's good for

Adam is the same for Eve? Except when Adam doesn't want her to have it because remember, he's in charge! God help us!

Well, I don't want to be accused of male bashing. So, I'd better remind you of the noble act of Adam at this point. Remember, God told me something very provocative about Adam. Adam did what he did for love. He didn't want to lose Eve even if it meant that he died with her. This is why Jesus is called the second Adam (I Cor 15:45). As Jesus said, there is no greater love than this (John 15:13). If this is so, then this makes Adam a nobler being than Eve might want to believe. I had a male friend who asked me if I ever wondered what would have happened if Adam had said no to Eve. My friend asked me if I thought Adam could have become Eve's Christ or savior. Maybe he did. You think this is why Jesus came in a male body? Did you think God had to come in a male's body? Is anything too hard for the Lord, is the hand of the Lord short that he cannot save (Isa 59:1)? Remember God could have done this any way He wanted. What we should always be asking ourselves is, why did God do it this way? Exploring God's action by asking this question reveals details buried for the child of God who is determined to know the truth (2 Tim 2:15). It is always rewarded!

What other god, in this world, speaks directly to Eve's redemption? Of all the religions I've studied, Eve is considered a sub-set of Adam with very little promises of redemption made to her. If anything is offered to her, she is paired with Adam for her salvation. Of all the religions in the world, who is for Eve?

I'm not going to bother naming any other religions because all of them have this same stance pertaining to Eve. The Jewish religion is the basis of Christianity therefore inclusive of the foundation of Christianity that speaks to Eve's particular situation; these being the only religion on this planet addressing the peculiarity of Eve's salvation, that I can find. For the God of the Old Testament, or Tunakh, has hidden in the Word what He thinks of women. These truths only come to the surface as we are ready to accept them. An example of this would be the daughters of Zelophehad (Num 27:1-11). These women demanded what was rightfully theirs even though the patriarchy had not considered them. You think this situation only came to God's mind when Moses brought it before God? The scriptures say that God knows what we need before we know (Mat 6:8) yet Jesus tells us to ask and we shall receive (Luke 11:9). Why do we need to ask if God already knows what we need? Could it be that God is waiting on us to know that we need something? If this is so, what other freedoms or gifts lie in the scriptures belonging to us, or to Eve especially, that we have not taken hold of because we have not pushed out or pressed into the Word (Luke 16:16, Mk 5:27)?

Do you ever give thought to the balancing act God must perform to keep us where we need to be until Jesus came and comes especially after the Spirit became available? With the introduction of the Holy Spirit, now mankind would show variations of, for lack of a better term, being in the Spirit and with greater possibilities of perversities in the flesh. Now the lies can cut deeper because we are open to the Spirit.

Before the Holy Spirit became available, our dull minds could accept the animal sacrifices as 'good enough' but we are able to know better now. This is why understanding Eve's situation is important. It will cause you to ask God about the differences in the law pertaining to men and women for the obliteration of that particular sin that must be dealt with in the conscience (Rom 2:15, 2 Tim 1:3).

I wondered about the differences and I asked God did He really think of women as second-class beings or are we subdued because we are dull in spirit? Is this why Satan was able to get through by using Eve? Are you mad at Eve more than with Adam because she sinned first? When I asked God all these questions, His answer to me is, while multi-layered and what I cannot concisely express, is contained in this book.

C. THE PATRIARCHY IN THE BOUNDS OF THE MATRIARCHY

As I said before the strength of the patriarchy lies in the foundational order of the paradigm. In other words, in the ideology of might makes right and the submissiveness of women. Since this paradigm is unilaterally worldwide, it is a God inspired system. This makes a broad statement about a matriarchy. A matriarchy would be detrimental to mankind. How do I know this? I know this because God didn't choose it. Moreover, history shows that as the patriarchy gets weaker, women in the paradigm get stronger; this in turn, allows another stronger form of the patriarchy that is more oppressive to women to develop and eventually usurp the weaker form of the paradigm. We have been living this cycle since we have been recording history. This is fundamentally through history, how governments are toppled.

The ills or blessing of the paradigm doesn't lie in the system but rather in the integrity of those meting out the system. The limitations of this paradigm also lie in the limitation of those meting out the system. Likewise, the strengths of the paradigm have its limitations in the rudiments for whom the system is designed.

To expound on this, we can look at the strengths of Adam that remained even after the Fall, although perverted. These strengths, one can observe, are fundamental design functions. For instance, Adam is physically stronger than Eve. Adam is the one who fathers the children. Adam views situations through the lens of less emotion than Eve when compared. Therefore, the patriarchy requires one to be the strongest and more emotionless relative to Eve and finally not primarily attached to the day-to-day activities required to develop the family or rear children.

So, the patriarchy allows, even expects, Eve to be weaker than Adam; and she physically is. The patriarchy expects that Eve will express herself in an emotional way rather than through logic; most often she does. Finally, the patriarchy expects Eve to do nothing more than the day-to-day activities required to rear children; and her body and mental disposition are designed for this task.

I have to say here that we are not to compare ourselves to each other as Paul says (2 Cor 10:12) because God designs as He wills. However, we don't seem to be able to help ourselves. It always seems to look greener on the other side of the fence. This is the beginning of our self-dissatisfaction. We rarely realize this as we fight to change the system to our liking. Once changed, we long for the old ways because peace does not come from the environment in which we live. Peace is within us if we have it at all. So, we chase this endless cycle until the Seed comes.

The attributes I listed above that seem to be the foundational pillars of the patriarchy are not negative or positive attributes. They simply exist. We attribute the various connotations from our sinful point of view. Understanding how God views who and what we are, can allow us to accept ourselves and exist contently in any paradigm.

The directive God gives Eve within the paradigm is fundamental to her existence, that is to say she just needs to bear children. Well, she was going to do that anyway if she was going to participate in this life at all. So, God couldn't have made it simpler for her. I do believe that God was speaking this obvious directive to her male counterpart though, to define her job in his mind. Remember this is necessary before he can move forward. It gives him direction in what to expect.

As Eve 'occupies until I come' (Luke 19:13), she has to learn obedience through submissiveness, like someone else we know (Heb 5:8). This submissiveness carries a great burden because within her submissiveness lies a responsibility that carries the weight of the whole world. She must give the necessary nourishment in due season for the baby to survive (Mat 24:45-51).

So as Paul says, 'stand fast in the liberty' (Gal 5:1) but continue to wait on the Lord for continual renewed strength to be submissive (Isa 40:31). Remember that accepting submissiveness doesn't mean accepting abuse. The more I study the patriarchy, the more I see that with the limitation God is dealing with in us because of sin, the more I see that this system was designed to protect us from ourselves. Yes, even women!

If you can't see this, just trust God until you can.

CHAPTER III

PRESS IN AND TAKE IT BY FORCE

A. THE COST OF SELF-AWARENESS

So, what now? Surprisingly (or rather, unsurprisingly) the way forward for Eve lies in Jesus' example. For He said, "I have not come to destroy but to fulfill" (Mat 5:17). As Eve embraces her new found freedom in Christ, she must obey the law for the church's sake. For we still are waiting until the Seed should come for the second time. This is the cost of self-awareness, sacrifice. For, indeed, the foundation of the patriarchy rest on Eve's shoulders; on Eve's submission. Even the purity of this paradigm is judged solely on the chastity of women. Remember the woman brought before Jesus that was caught in the act of adultery (John 8:4)? There was no thought to bring the man with her to entrap Jesus even though the law said both were to be stoned (Lev 20:10). This attitude is not exclusive to men but we all condemn the guilty and make absolutions for our own sins as if God will forgive us but not the others.

However, the emphasis we are working to understand, in this book, is this interaction between men and women. This is important to understand because the difference between what is necessary in the paradigm we live in and what is accentuated by sin in the flesh, is also the difference between the law given by God that speaks to the submissiveness of women versus the enslaving of women. Knowing this difference allows women to assert themselves without challenging manhood, like the 5 daughters of Zelophehad (Num 27:1-8).

Submitting does not mean that women must endure abuse but it does mean there will be sacrifices to make. This shouldn't shock any woman. Women have been making sacrifices throughout history anyway. Now, with this different way of looking at our situation, we should be able to inject more of the Love of God in our actions. Let's let God be God so we can get this thing over with and start enjoying eternity!

There was an interesting study I read that concluded as women gain equal rights, that society, as a whole, diminishes. I believe this study was done in the 1990s and at that time I was studying world history. This particular study, documented the progression of various cultures understanding that all cultures have their bases as patriarchal. It was the novelty of the study to track this progression by the interaction of the women in that culture that made the study unique. The outcome of this study didn't surprise me because I had already notice that the basis of society, was mainly to nurture the male psyche.

I just didn't know why until now. Men seem to need to differentiate what women do from what men are supposed to do to ground themselves. This is the thinking of the natural man which thinking is broken by sin but still is something that we must accept until the restoration. As we press into the Spirit and take it by force, women are strengthened by the Spirit to submit and men press in to be freed from thinking that women constantly challenge them while exerting their God-given rights.

So, what is the cost of our self-awareness? How does one know the need for freedom without knowing slavery? According to Paul, this is why the law was introduced. The law became our schoolmaster to bring us to Christ (Gal 3:24). Under the law, women learn to submit. However, the Word frees; if the Son therefore shall make you free, you shall be free indeed (John 8:36). Christ has redeemed us from the curse of the law, being made a curse for us...and there is neither Jew nor Greek, there is neither bond or free, there is neither male nor female: for you are all one in Christ Jesus (Gal 3:13, 28). But the paradigm remains until the Seed returns because remember, Christ came to fulfill not to destroy (Mat 10:28). The cost of our self-awareness was every drop of blood coming from Christ's body. This alone, should give us a hint of the importance God put on this sacrifice in using such a priceless commodity. The blood of God, the blood of Christ.

Now, when we think of this sacrifice, we seem to exclude women; I mean outside of the childbearing thing. We don't tend to think that all of what Jesus did was to free women too. Even the progressive ideas in the Bible must contend with the patriarchal slant. This is where we press in to understand what God is saying to women. No matter what men understand, it will be for men. This is also true with women. When we allow each other to be who God made us to be, then we shall be one in the spirit. The unity that is only in Christ will show itself, and greater works then these (which Christ did) will be done through us (John 14:12).

The reason why we haven't seen these 'greater works' is because they require a unity that, I know, will be present at the end times. This unity will require the male Adam and the female Adam to come together as they did in the garden. Therefore, Eve must submit to see this. The test is as simple as this for her because this is her point of failure. What does the scripture say of Christ as He submitted (John 19:11, Phil 2:8)? Christ passed his test knowing that God could change things or save Him from the cross but he allowed time and actions to unfold as God saw fit. Jesus was doing God's will just as Eve should have said to the serpent, 'although I want to eat of this tree, God's will, is not for me to eat of this tree; and it is not what I will but what God wills.' Jesus trusted God! Eve must trust God also!

This test was why the two trees were in the garden in the first place. What is amazing, is that God has produced the same outcome for us as if Adam took from the tree of life. We end up back in the garden with life eternal and in the presence of God (Rev 22:14). I wish we could have experienced the outcome of taking from the Tree of Life first. I don't know about you but I could have done without the suffering and dying part to become a new creature in Christ. I bet Jesus hoped the same thing.

So, from the time of the fall of man up till now, we have lived this cycle of death in our bodies as well as our civilizations. We can always say, "we have been here before." Truly there is nothing new under the sun (Ecc 1:9). When God provided a sure way out of this cycle of death, when the Holy Spirit became available, we still perpetuated this cycle. For the antagonism between men and women to pervade even after the inception of the Holy Spirit, is truly astonishing. Indeed, Christ has allowed this for nearly two thousand years now. Let's look at this cycle as it pertains to men and women with examples from the Bible.

When I say that we have been here before, I mean the cycle for women in any new-to-old civilization. One can see this same cycle in secular historical writings as well as in the Bible. To our shame in the church, because the Holy Spirit is available, we can see various stages of this cycle in the now, as there seem to be no end to it. Even so come Lord Jesus!

The cycle begins with the extreme oppression towards women. You know what I mean, women have no say in anything nor are they considered any more than a possession. Any atrocity against them is considered only as a loss of property. The regulation of male behavior is done thru the various laws or limitations put on women. For example, women will be subject to a certain dress code to inhibit desire in men. In breaking these restrictions women are held responsible or guilty for any infraction that comes of this. However, the men, if considered guilty, are considered less guilty even though Jesus said, "if a man looks on a woman to lust after her, he has committed adultery with her already in his heart." (Mat 5:28) This signifies that we are all responsible for our own thoughts to maintain self-control.

These ideas, while some are in flux, seem to be fostered by the need for control as I said in the previous chapters, that came out of the curse. This is not hidden from men. A poignant example of this is the story of how Ester becomes queen. Even though Ester serves God's purpose, pay attention to what is said and the limitations God has in working with sinful flesh. The story goes that the King got drunk out of his mind and as men do, they got into a contest about who has the prettiest girl. As the king is bragging on all the stuff he owned and queen Vashti, not to her glory but to his, he orders her to appear before his court. According to the text, he ordered her to appear wearing the royal crown only. In other words, to be nude to show off her beauty. She refused, so the king banished her. Listen to the words his counselors used to explain to him why he needed to banish the queen (Ester 1:22):

The king asks, "What shall we do unto the queen Vashti according to law, because she hath not performed the commandment of the king Ahasuerus by the chamberlains?"

16 And Memucan answered before the king and the princes, Vashti the queen hath not done wrong to the king only, but also to all the princes, and to all the people that are in all the provinces of the king Ahasuerus.

17 For this deed of the queen shall come abroad unto all women, so that they shall despise their husbands in their eyes, when it shall be reported, The king Ahasuerus commanded Vashti the queen to be brought in before him, but she came not.

18 Likewise shall the ladies of Persia and Media say this day unto all the king's princes, which have heard of the deed of the queen. Thus, shall there arise too much contempt and wrath.

19 If it please the king, let there go a royal commandment from him, and let it be written among the laws of the Persians and the Medes, that it be not altered, That Vashti come no more before king Ahasuerus; and let the king give her royal estate unto another that is better than she.

20 And when the king's decree which he shall make shall be published throughout all his empire, (for it is great,) all the wives shall give to their husbands honour, both to great and small.

21 And the saying pleased the king and the princes; and the king did according to the word of Memucan:

22 For he sent letters into all the king's provinces, into every province according to the writing thereof, and to every people after their language, that every man should bear rule in his own house, and that it should be published according to the language of every people.

Does this sound like these men don't know what they are doing? Why would there be wrath if they believed they are making reasonable requests? To publish this quickly and to all, is to confirm their control over women. Also, to find a woman better than Vashti, implies to find a woman willing to submit. While under these conditions Ester shines in her compliance and saves her people, there is something noble in Vashti that should not go unnoticed. Ester represents obeying God in an unfair system expecting Him to deliver her in His time frame. Vashti represents women fighting their way out of an unfair system outside of God's time frame. These two women demonstrate exactly what this book is trying to display. They were both subject to the paradigm but only one was exalted.

Since the law and the prophets are not going anywhere until Jesus returns, if Vashti had prevailed, where was she going to go? What was she going to be? Remember, submitting doesn't mean submitting to abuse, although it may cost you. The men indeed would have revolted and if the women continued to fight back, what do you think the outcome would have been? It would have been as it has been since recorded time. This is the point where the cycle begins again. Either the patriarchy clamps down and reinforces the system or it gets weaker by the rule of women (because this takeover cannot be done in the love walk) and another civilization, at the height of the patriarchy, comes to dominate. Although we are encouraged to press into what is right (Luke 16:16), God reinforces the current structure, so Eve must continue to wait on the Lord (Psa. 27:14) to be free indeed (John 8:36).

This is what makes now so exciting. We are at the point of exchange in the cycle again in the world. If this is God's final time, Eve will make that choice that hasn't been made yet and wasn't available to her until Jesus came. This means that there is the possibility that the cycle will change making things ready for the appearing of Jesus. The scriptures state that in the end times God will pour out his spirit on ALL flesh; and your sons and your daughters will prophesy...also upon the servants an upon the handmaids will I pour out my spirit... (Joel 2:28, 29; Acts 2:17,18). Remember God can do this any way He wants. He seems to be going out of His way to include Eve in these scriptures. Why? When He poured out His spirit to alleviate Moses' responsibility, no women were called out (Ex 18:25, Num 11:16). Do you think He needs to here, at the end times? Has something changed? Does Eve have a job to do that she could not fulfill before the Seed came, before the spirit became available? Eve, absolutely needs restoration for the whole to be restored (Rom 11:16)!

You might think that men fight this spiritual equality of women because they are afraid of being controlled by women. I think there is a little of this with not wanting to be considered weak like women are perceived. This attitude is displayed if men are bested by women in any way. They will get teased by other men. I don't know if this is still a thing but when was a little girl, I remember in the schoolyard, boys getting into fights because one of them called the other a 'girl'. Another instance that would cause other boys to tease each other was if a girl knocked a boy down in some kind of scuffle. The other boys would tease him by saying, 'you let a girl beat you.' These were fighting words as far as little boys were concerned. This is not a new sentence of great dishonor from a man's point of view. Look at this example from Judges 9:52-54:

52 And Abimelech came unto the tower, and fought against it, and went hard unto the door of the tower to burn it with fire.

53 And a certain woman cast a piece of a millstone upon Abimelech's head, and all to brake his skull.

54 Then he called hastily unto the young man his armourbearer, and said unto him, Draw thy sword, and slay me, that men say not of me, A women slew him. And his young man thrust him through, and he died.

I think this says it all.

I cannot ever remember an example of girls getting into a fight because one call the other a 'boy.' This is not to say we haven't moved towards this direction in the now, but as I was growing up, this seems to not be a thing for girls.

So, as we come to this axis point; what will we become? Do we even have any examples of what Adam and Eve were before sin? She was indeed a help meet for him but what does that mean? How did they work together? I think we are about to find out. The cost of this knowledge for both is self-awareness; acknowledging and owning their own part in sin; no longer blaming the other.

B. THE NEW LAW IN CHRIST

Did you know that Jesus even expressed the same desire that Eve does? The desire to be free of a system that God has allowed to be the bases of this plan even though it only leads to death. When God told Abraham to sacrifice Isaac (Gen 22:8), this put into motion what would happen in the future when Jesus appeared on earth. Yet even knowing this, in the garden, Jesus pleaded with God not to go through with it (Mat 26:39). What made this request perfect? In the end, Jesus wanted not what he wanted but what God wanted. Paul writes in I Cor 13:7 that love bears all things. Doesn't this by reflex sound like a selfless mother? No matter what situation her kid gets into, he or she is perfect in the mother's eyes. I am trying to express to Eve that she inherently has what is needed to press through, like Jesus did. The result will be the true expression of the Love of God in you. You must walk in the Spirit and not want the things of the flesh (Gal 5:16). Throughout this paradigm, you have been, you are and you will bear all things! However, not for yourself, choose to let God be God, for God has already set certain things in motion and as the situation unfolds, you must want to do what God wants done. Do not repeat Eve's mistake. Do not try to take matters into your own hands. Do not repeat Eve's sin.

At this point, I need to make that plead for you to accept Jesus Christ as your Lord and Savior if you haven't already. This will be the only way for you succeed; you need the Holy Spirit to have the strength to make the right choice in the Walk, not to mention, to have life everlasting. Most of the time, God send me to those who have already accepted Jesus as Lord. I can only think of a hand full of times where I ever spoke to an unsaved person about Christ. I am hoping against hope that this writing goes out to all, therefore I must assume some level of newness, on the reader's part, when talking about Christ. To accept Christ, you must say out loud, that you do accept Him as Lord and savior and believe, in your heart, that He has saved you (Rom 10:9, 10). Then God will take it from there. Continue to be open minded and obedient as He directs your life. Watch what happens!

From a woman's point of view, as I have stated before, there is no other religion that I know of, that exalts a woman to be equal to a man while accepting their differences except the Christian religion. This of itself makes it a religion for Eve.

So, knowing that the paradigm of the patriarchy is here to stay, and that there are some that still must "enter into" the rest of God (Heb 4:5, 9, 10), all of what Eve is, as God see her, should be hidden in the paradigm until the time this information needs to be revealed. God the Father and Jesus would use this notion that Eve is not useful in the patriarchy, in a particular way, to conceal Eve's purpose. You will be astonished by what jumps out at you in the Bible when this truth is explored. For example, did you know that the genealogy of Jesus in the book of Luke is from Mary, not Joseph (Luk 3:23-38)? If you compare the genealogy of Jesus in Mathew (Mat 1:16) and Luke, you will find that Luke branches off to Mary's bloodline rather than incorporate Joseph's bloodline. When God makes an ascertain, the enemy is always there to try and stop it somehow. So, when God tells David that the Messiah will come through his line, the enemy began to attack David's lineage. The male lineage through David was cursed thru Jeconiah (Jer 22:30). This curse would have prohibited the blessing of the Messiah to come through David lineage. I bet the enemy though he had succeeded but God had a hidden plan. Eve.

Although Joseph (Mary's husband) was of the cursed bloodline of David, he was still the legal guardian of Jesus by marriage or by the law; but he was not Jesus' father. Mary, as a descendant of David's line but not cursed, fulfilled the promise through David's bloodline. This also speaks to what was added to the law by the request of the five daughters of Zelophehad (num 27:1-8). For a cursed bloodline is like having no sons to carry on in the bloodline, so the responsibility would lay on the only ones left in the bloodline; the females. The bloodline thru Eve. So, by this stipulation added to the law for fathers with no sons, Mary was able to help fulfill the promise of the Messiah thru David's bloodline.

If this paradigm, the patriarchy, is not what God wants but must use, you might wonder how does the Holy Spirit change Eve to help her regain her original status? You may even wonder what her original status was because this is blurred under the patriarchy. If you think walking in the

Spirit for Eve is just obeying her other half then we do indeed need to explore her original status to understand who she is.

Here are some questions to consider. What was the intend when God created Adam? What was Adam supposed to be? If he wasn't perfect in his original form, why did God need to split Adam in two? Since Adam is not the beginning of God's creation, could Adam be another hidden plan of God, directed towards the beings that existed before us? What was the mind of Eve like in the love walk, which was before they sinned? What was she supposed to be doing? Well, the scriptures say that she was supposed to be a help meet for him (Gen 2:18). So, she would have been someone that he could bounce his ideas off; they would enjoy each other's presence by being creative together. He would say, let's do this and she would say let's add that. It would be kind of like what God said in Gen 1:26 when They created man. It was by consensus. Anything they did would be a collaborative creative act, just like making a baby.

Well, when sin entered and Eve is now walking in the flesh, the collaborative act becomes a conflict and a test of wills as they both seek after a selfish gain. In the natural, Eve wants what she wants and to be the object of his desire. When she doesn't get what she wants, her natural inclination is to tear him down even though she was designed to build him up. Indeed, the balance for this, that God seems to have put in place, is her submission; which denies her wants and makes her chase after his desire. This describes our lives since time has been recorded. If there is nothing more to life and love than this, we might as well eat, drink and be merry for tomorrow we die (I Cor 15:32). But thanks be to God, which has not left us in this dark existence, we have hope of a higher life (I Cor 15:57, Isa 55:9, Phil 2:5, 6).

A friend of mine related a story about his marriage that I think exemplify what I'm trying to demonstrate here. He expressed to his wife that he wanted a man cave. He told me that he could see the hurt in her eyes as if she was thinking, "why would you need any time away from me?" He went on to tell me that he tried to explain to her that his request had nothing to do with being away from her; it was just that he wanted a place when he could spread out without intruding in her space and she wouldn't have to search for her things in the mist of his things. Although this sounded reasonable, the more he tried to explain, the less it sounded like something harmless to her. He told me that this situation turned into an argument but in the end, he got his man cave.

One day, after a year or so of having his man cave, he was looking for something and came across one of her earrings that was in a place that it would have had to have been placed there. In other words, her ear ring could not have gotten there accidentally. He knew that she put it there. He knew that she could only live with this situation as long as she knew that something of hers was in his man cave. I asked him what he did about this. He told me that he wanted to stay married, so he left the ear ring there and said nothing about it to her. This is a good example of the part of the curse on Eve; that her desire will be for him. This surprisingly is a reoccurring theme in the bible where the male counterpart must go off to do something without the beloved or bride and she becomes jealous. In Song of Solomon, the male lover goes off to complete other tasks as she searches for him (Song 3:2, 5:2,3) and the ultimate example is Jesus Himself, going off to tend to his other sheep (John 10:16) and leaving His newly formed church in Acts 1:9, as we all wait for the call, "the bridegroom cometh!" (Mat 25:6). Every example seems to point out tasks that need to be completed to prepare for the beloved or bride but could this also be a test for Eve not to react jealously?

In the natural, this infuriates Eve because she wants him to think of her as his one and only. She cannot accept that he can go off to do other things and not be thinking about her until he finishes whatever needs to be done while still loving her. In her reality, he consumes her thoughts, so she should consume his thoughts. However, Adam cannot. His reaction to this part of the curse is that he can only rule over her (Gen 3:16). In the faith walk, he will still need to leave to prepare. So, either way Eve will have to deal with this by exercising at least one of the fruits of the spirit, self-control.

Eve in the love walk, will wait patiently for his return. This should give you a new outlook on the scripture where God says, "they that wait on the Lord shall renew their strength..." (Isa 40:31). This is an act of faith.

C. PRESERVING THE ESSENCE OF EVE (OLD TESTAMENT)

As I said before, we must ask ourselves what Eve was supposed to be doing relative to Adam before the fall? Was her only job to bearing children and help Adam? The best way to answer this question is to note how Eve is restricted in the patriarchy and to look at what Jesus restores to her in his coming.

Eve is not allowed to minister in the temple or preach/teach to the congregation. She is not allowed to be a priest or administer any offering. However, when we look at the proverb 31 woman, she is busy and working. This woman looks more like today's woman. From the description of what this woman does, I'm beginning to believe the women of the turn of the century or the woman that had everything like the large house, servants, nannies were more of a trophy that men could brag about rather than the societal norm of the past. This was not good for the women of that time because she was idle with a mind comparable to Adam that can imagine anything. With all her duties taken care, of course she would want to study and involve herself in the world around her only to find out that she couldn't because she lacked one body part. No one saw women suffrage coming?

Yet there is a hint of who she is in the Old Testament. Let's pull out some examples that don't quite fit the patriarchal mold, from the

Old Testament. Women that seem to be in roles that we are told are forbidden for women. In every major movement or progression of God, He leaves Himself a witness of a woman in a pivotal position critical for the next step in His plan with a subtlety that almost dismisses her involvement in the situation. If you are with me so far, you are thinking about certain women in the Old Testament that get mentioned in sermons as good examples of submissive women, like Sarah, Ruth or Ester and we will discuss these women along with the few others. The point will be to display them in a slightly different light. To show that God placed them there as examples of returning to the unity of Adam for our present time because this type of thinking would have been considered blasphemous in their time.

Well, we have already talked about Eve, so let's move on to the next woman in a pivotal time, Sarah. She is in the dispensational time of promise (Scofield Bible, pg. 20, 24), representing a time of grace from God and as the "freewoman" (Gal 4:22-31). Can you see any of these plans happening without her? Likewise, she wouldn't be able to participate without Abraham's obedience. This is the unity of the two Adams back into one Adam that we are moving towards; the Alpha and Omega. These examples were there before, we just had our attention on who shouldn't be doing what or who is in charge of what, (I Cor 11:9-11). However, as God opens our minds to His larger plan, we begin to see how we must again become one in Him.

So, Sarah believed God and Isaac is born. There are other subtleties in this story that are worth noting. As Sarah makes a declaration (Gen 21:10-12) that God tells Abraham to obey the voice of his wife (remember Adam got in trouble for doing this), yet Paul calls it out as the scriptures had spoken it (Gal 4:30) rather than Sarah. This subtlety deflects her importance unless you are looking at who was used in this instance.

There is a small but interesting blurb about the sister of Moses and Aaron, Miriam. The first notable thing is that she was called a prophetess but the scriptures doesn't record anything in particular that she did in the name of the Lord (Mic 6:4). After the Egyptians were drowned in the sea, she led the woman in praising God for His deliverance (Ex 15:19-21). This may seem like a small thing but we all know the power of praise. Therefore, services always start off with praise and worship to get our minds in the right place to receive from God. Did she deserve equal status with Aaron for some specific reason? Could her status be simply due to her position in the family? If this is true, this hasn't been true for any other woman; or has it (I Cor 7:14)? Could it be that Paul hit on something? If it is not possible to have one side of a union sanctified and the other unsanctified, then they both must be sanctified before God for his purpose to unfold. I ask you again, what was Eve made to be as a help meet for Adam? Part of the answer must lie in the male Adam's responsibility that God gave him.

If Miriam's responsibility was negligible, her words would be treated as a minor infraction. However, when she and Aaron spoke against Moses, although God was displeased with both,

Miriam was punished more severely than Aaron (Num 12). I have read commentaries that believe Aaron could not be punished because he wore the robes of the priesthood. Could it even be just as plausible that Miriam stoked, if not begin, the words against Moses? Most often, women don't appreciate the power of persuasion we have to incite or defuse a situation. Could Miriam have noticed a little attitude in Aaron about Moses and help the situation grow into something that God would not let go unchecked for it would have greatly interfered with His plans. I believe, because of this ability women have, God approached Miriam for her words although she and Aaron were one in this attitude.

I think there is a grave lesson here for women with men, in whatever type of relationship, that have some kind of position in the church. Whether your male counterpart is right or wrong, you'd better keep your opinion to yourself, keep your mouth shut (because of your power of persuasion) and support him by praying for God to lead you both in His will.

We already talked about the daughters of Zelophehad, how their exertion of their rights allowed Mary's bloodline to be acceptable for Jesus to be called the son of David to inherit the promise from God of the throne. Ester, we talked about as a woman functioning in the constraints of the patriarchy in comparison to Vashti; showing that this obedience facilitates the plan of God. This is in line with the Proverbs 31 woman (Prov 31:12 - 31). This woman is a business man. She buys and sell as she cares for her household. This is a very different picture of what our industrial generation was told a good housewife is. As I said before, no wonder women suffrage occurred. Women are capable of so much more. To just keep a house clean, children fed and tend to a husband doesn't even push up against feeling half as useful as a woman can be.

We cannot talk about the great women of the Old Testament without mentioning Debra (Judges 4). She was not only a prophetess but the only female judge Israel ever had. This whole chapter in Judges depicts women in the act of deliverance and in a women's point of view of the battle. Remember, God can do this any way He wants. For God to make even one judge in Israel a woman, is a statement. The ramifications of what God allows here are much deeper than we will touch on but for now let's list the obvious. The first thing we should notice is that the scriptures imply that she ruled passively sitting under a tree and the people came to her. Also, Israel experienced a period of peace just as they did under the other judges and then fell back into sin. So, Debra offered no lasting peace like any male judge. Another thing to notice is that Debra did not offer to go with Barak, he insisted that she go. What I'm trying to point out here is a woman in a traditional male position straddling the line between the social mores of what is expected of a man and woman; like today's woman, working as the only female in leadership in a company.

So, the men fought the battle but the women set the tone. As the enemy of Israel ran from the battle, a woman killed him (Judges 4:21). In the next chapter of Judges, Deborah composes a song about the battle. In it she considers what the enemy of Israel mother must be thinking about his not returning from battle yet. I doubt a man writing these lyrics would even think of something like this.

What other statements do you think God is making by allowing a female judge and prophetess to deliver Israel?

The last woman of the Old Testament that I would like to mention is Rahab but not for the reason you might think. We all know she hid the spies (Judges 2:1-21) and saved the life of her family but did you know that she is in the bloodline of Jesus by Ruth (Heb 11:31, Mat 1:5)? So, when the Pharisees accused Jesus of being a Samaritan and having a devil, Jesus only denied having a devil (John 8:48) because He knew his bloodline.

Well, this leads us to the women in the New Testament and how God's plan is literally exposed through Paul's writings but we have taken no notice of this until now.

CHAPTER IV

RESTORING THE ESSENCE OF EVE (NEW TESTAMENT)

A. THE RESTORATION AND HIDDEN MEMORIAL TO WOMEN IN THE NEW TESTAMENT

Now we come to the whole purpose of this book. All the scriptures and examples that came before this was to finally converge to this one point. To prove through scripture that Eve is just as much a priest after the order of Melchizedek as Adam. While their responsibilities are different, their order of relevance and holiness are equal by the Lord, in the Lord (Mat 10:25).

As we move from the Old Testament to the New Testament and the Seed has come, we see God restoring these responsibilities back to both Adams. God tells us that His word will not return to him void (Isa 55:11) and that He is the beginning and end of things (Rev 1:8). Therefore, restoration is the obvious next step in His plan for mankind. The restoration of both Adams was finished on the cross, the only thing left to happen is the unfolding of time towards the Omega.

The way His plan unfolds, upholds the structure of society before the Seed came. In other words, as Jesus said, "Think not that I have come to destroy...I come to fulfill" (Mat 5:17). This means, among other things, that God will not change the social constructs that we are familiar with, but rather use them. God will not undo the patriarchy but use it even though we are new creatures in Him not subject to the law (Rom 8:2, Gal 3:13). We are still, as Paul puts it "in this body of death" (Rom 7:24) so we are still subject to the pulls of sin while having a weapon against sin, the Holy Spirit, until we are clothed upon (II Cor 5:2). Not to mention, we still have a job to do. That is to help bring the other sons of glory to Him (Heb 2:10, Mk 16:15). We could not relate to them if God changed the only environment we've known. After we are given our new bodies, do you think this is what the eventual new heaven and new earth are about (Rev 21:1)?

From the beginning of Eve's sin up until now, God has been unfolding a plan for her in a very quiet and subtle way. Allowing His back turned to her, as Jesus turned from Peter when he contradicted Him, to appear to be a sign of her unworthiness. This tactic God uses, covers her importance in His plan while maintaining her humility. This was very necessary before the Seed came because she had no power not to continue in the same sin as Eve. However, now she can withstand the Devil's whispers by the Holy Spirit (Eph 6:13).

Now we move from the initial point of Eve's sin and what God promised her in the restoration. He promised her that her Seed would restore them to the garden and God's favor. This brings us to the Eve that would materialize this promise, Mary, Jesus' mother. Some of the sermons I heard about her, paint her as a very pious and obedient woman. I must agree with this and imagine her as devoted to God by wisdom with insight that she could not share. As God prepares her for her mission, even before she realizes that she is chosen, He had to endow her with some measure of the Spirit (like he did to the prophets of old) to be successful. Could it have taken the four thousand years from Eve's sin to put women in this low estate so they could be used by God (Luke 1:48)?

The little that the scriptures say about Mary's personality, implies that she was discerning, thoughtful and did not share her insights with others (Luke 2:19). I suspect that she would not find anyone to be able to share what god was doing in her life because of her unique calling. Could this be part of the silent battle of women? The enmity God put between the woman and the devil (Gen 3:15)? Have you ever wondered what Jesus spoke about when He was alone with just women? Do you assume that the exact Word He preaches to Adam is the same Word He preaches to Eve (I Cor 9:22)?

If Mary were a man facilitating a great work of God as she did, she would have been called a prophet or apostle. This is not to say that she is not a prophet or an apostle but just not thought of as one because she is a woman. Yet she acknowledged that all generations would call her blessed (Luke 1:48). A thing which God had to balance against Mary being worshiped as a god. This is the very sin Eve tried to commit.

So, we can now see the parallel of God's plan being worked out with Eve as center stage through Mary. Adam has his role to play from the banishment of the garden until now, but at this point, the promises to Eve began to play out. I believe the blessing spoken of women, through childbearing in I Tim 2:15 was accomplished through Mary when she gave birth to Jesus and is no longer a standalone blessing. Now, is there a continued blessing in just having a child? Yes, of course but this is a natural consequence in life and this is not what God was saying to Eve. I cannot find a scripture or passage in the bible, so far, that implies that Eve would not want to have children because of sin. So, to assume that God said this to her about childbearing for any reason other than to promote life until the Seed should come, makes no sense.

While we are talking about Mary, we cannot forget the mother of the herald God sent to let everyone know that the time is near for the Seed to appear, John the Baptist. John's mother, Elisabeth, was a type of Sarah (Luke 1:18). You think God uses this age tactic of childbearing through an old woman to show everyone that He is the God over time also? It is noteworthy that those things that can appear usual or normal to mankind, God sometimes make these things appear as curses to augment its importance (Rom 7:13) just as Paul says that God does the opposite in I Cor 12:23 to make certain things seem sanctified that we despise. For example, Elisabeth says in Luke 1:25 that God took away her reproach among men of being childless by giving her John; especially in her old age. The example of the less honorable being bestowed with more honor is Eve, herself.

Let's move to our next New Testament example of God working part of His plan through Eve. Let's look at the actions of Anna in Luke 2:24. As Mary and Joseph bring Jesus into the temple to perform the ritual in the Law of Moses for the first-born son, two prophets meet them; Simeon meets them first and then Anna comes to them by the Spirit afterwards to agree with the prophetic word given to Mary and Joseph by Simeon. This is a great example of the male and female priest acting as one. So, were there no other male priest moved by the Spirit to come and greet the child Jesus? Do you think this is just a coincidence that Anna was there? We all know the scripture that says what happens when two are agreed (Mat 18:19). Did this agreement require male and female concurrence? Why? We know coincidence and accidents do not happen to God and that we can only agree in accordance with His will (Rom 8:28).

I note again, the subtext of a particular struggle directed towards women when Simeon mentions this as it relates to the Woman, Mary, "a sword shall pierce through thy own soul also" (Luke 2:35).

There are many examples throughout the Bible, like a scarlet thread that runs through God's narrative, demonstrating a pattern that God was and is working a particular action necessary towards Eve's restoration. I am not listing them all. Only the ones that can show what I mean. Sometimes, it is so blatant, one can wonder why we never saw it before now. Another example of this is the woman bound for 18 years, (Luke 13:12). Jesus could have said you are healed, like he did so many times or be it according to your faith but He didn't. He specifically called out the woman and said that she was free from her infirmity. Remember, God can do this any way He wants. This example is there for a reason. Was Jesus telling all women through this example that we are free from our enmity between us and Serpent (Gen 3:15)?

Now we come to one of my favorite stories in the Bible, the woman at the well, John 4:7-43. What's amazing about this story is that Jesus was waiting for her to come. You won't pick this up unless you have settled in your understanding that nothing by coincidence, happens to God. It is all planned out for our benefit (I Cor 10:11). So, she didn't just happen to show up at the well any more than Jesus just happened to be alone. He sent His disciples away so He could talk to this woman alone. Jesus had a ministry to this woman (just as the woman had a ministry from God) but He kept this hidden from His disciples. Why?

Jesus speaks or calls to her first. He knew she would not speak to him because she had been conditioned by social mores and knowing that Jews don't interact with Samarians. So, Jesus has to break the social norm to get her attention, just as He did with Peter with the unclean animals in the great sheet (Acts 11:5). Her first question to him is this very idea. How is He talking to me or asking anything of me, He's a Jew? Jesus uses this as His entrance to correct her thinking about God and educate her about who she is in God.

When I have heard preachers preaching on this passage, this is not the message conveyed. Their preaching is all about her being a sinner and not a Jew but still having salvation. While this is true, the part left out is what Jesus is saying to Eve at this point. Truly, I didn't expect any male preacher to hit on this point but some have, to my surprise. I wasn't expecting this because they were male and because these actions of Jesus are particular to Eve's situation. I'm sure there are aspects to being a male that I cannot identify with and would not know or understand, however, as I said before, the system we live in is designed to make male issues known and to mitigate the stifling issues of femininity from the male's perspective. Have you ever been to a revival and felt that the message was only for the men?

The first thing Jesus says to the woman at the well is: if you knew...you would ask of Me, (John 4:10). The woman, limited to her environment, wonders how he could give her anything. This is where keeping the system we live in or familiar constructs or the environment the same helps. It allows God to condescend to us; after all, His ways are higher than ours (Isa 55:9).

However, it does appear that she had an inkling that Jesus might be talking about something else when she asks Him if He is greater than the fathers before her. Here Jesus gives her insight into a concept that had been hidden, living waters.

She has enough spiritual sense to accept this offer then Jesus brings her back to her environment by asking where she is in the law. She admits her true state and Jesus lets her know that He knows what she omitted. Faced with her sin exposed, she didn't try to blame someone else or try to defend herself nor did she get offended by Jesus' words but she showed that she was relying on God, as she understands Him, to vindicate herself. As a gentile, this is remarkable! She essentially says that when God comes, He will save me, no matter what. When our sin is exposed, we give off what is close to our heart. In other words, we show what we are in the inside. I can tell from this woman's response that she was thinking about God more than the average person and while she didn't live a godly life as the law defines it, there was still something in her that adhered to God. Jesus confirms that God will indeed save her, (John 4:23). Did you also notice that Jesus admits to her that He is the Messiah. In every other instance that I could find, Jesus either withheld this information or only admits it after someone said we know who you are.

The most amazing thing about this story that tell us what kind of woman this was, is the response of the whole city coming out to see Jesus at her word. If she was just a low-life individual or just a whore, would the whole city follow her to meet Jesus? This also implies that she must have preached from time to time in her own way about God even though her life wasn't a model of a pious woman. You know the old saying, don't judge a book by its cover.

Well, after this conversation with the woman,

Jesus is so excited, he can't eat when His disciples return with food. Here is another thing that might escape attention because Jesus was talking to a woman, the dissertation He gives about doing the will of Him who sent Him and the harvest makes the woman one that is sent, an apostle. So, was Paul truly the first one sent to the gentiles?

The next two examples really nailed Eve's particular sin or her enmity with Satan to the cross, for me, and showed me that God wanted to restore her to her original state. These examples are very subtle but powerful. A truth hiding in plain sight!

When the woman came in to Jesus with the alabaster box (Mat 26:7-13, Mk 14:3-9), and Jesus said she was preparing Him for His burial, this signified that she understood what Jesus was saying when He began to tell His disciples that He was about to be crucified (Luke 9:44, 45). Understand that this alabaster box represents a great value a woman can have in that culture. Its content was accumulated over time and was associated with her dowry. So, for her to break it open and use its contents on Jesus is for her to say that Jesus is the most important thing in her life. Remember that women are laden with the responsibility of maintaining the social customs in any culture. The purity of the culture rests on their submissiveness to the social mores. Since having this box is not a thing in our culture, it may be difficult to relate what she was sacrificing here. There is another story of a woman with an alabaster box (Luke 7:37, 38) coming to Jesus and wiping her tears off His feet with her hair. This is a separate story that shows the values of this box and that it was absolutely something women ascribed to have in that culture. However, Jesus did not say that this woman was preparing Him for His burial. So, this is a different story not to be confused with the woman who Jesus said was preparing Him for His burial.

As I said before and still must remind you, God can do His story or narrative any way He wants. He is not constrained or limited by what's happening in the story. He is developing the story. So, why do you think Jesus let the woman prepare Him for His burial rather than one of His disciples? Let me ask this another way, who is Jesus that His burial is important to the story? Jesus is the Passover lamb, right (Gen 22:8, Isa 53:7, John 1:36, 1 Peter 1:19, 1 Cor 5:7,) Who prepares the Passover lamb, according to the law, for sacrifice (Lev 5:12, 6:22, 29, 7:35; 2 Chron35:10-14)? As far as I know, it has never been called out in the Bible that the woman of the household sacrifices or prepares the Passover lamb for the family. Nor was there any female Levite sacrificing at the alter at any time. So, what is Jesus doing here with this woman? Is Jesus restoring her to her priesthood by allowing her to do what was denied to her after she sinned first (Gen 4:3-4)?

Could this be the memorial that Jesus was talking about? An act that signifies Eve's restoration that could only be accepted in our time because the Holy Spirit has had the perfect work of patience these two thousand years since Jesus' sacrifice (1 James 1:4)? Is this why Jesus memorializes her act? Not because it was just something nice, she did for Him but because this act represents something far more significant?

Well, let's look at the other act by a woman that also seems restorative. As I remind you once again, God can do this anyway He wants. I keep saying this because we as humans tend to think that things unfold for God as they unfold for us; as if God has no control over His day like we do not. We barely understand what happened to us yesterday much less know what's about to happen to us when we go out the door for the day. We expect to just go to work or get to where we are going but every day, we read stories about people who never make to their destinations. God doesn't experience this. God not only knows what will happen but He can also plan what will happen. God controls destiny. God is destiny.

Now we come to the next important piece of information Jesus tried to relay to His disciples, the fact that He would rise after three days from His burial (Mk 8:31). For the sake of proving who He is, one would think that this act would be the most significant act that would warrant confirmation by His disciples. Yet the only ones there to meet Jesus rising from His burial were women. The first to see Him was Mary Magdalene (Mk 16:9). This wasn't an accident! Like the incident where Jesus gives Peter a chance to vindicate himself after he denied knowing Jesus three times by asking him if he love Him three times (John 21:15-17), the woman at His rising is God giving Eve a chance to vindicate herself for denying the absolute deity of God first. She not only gets to acknowledge God in Christ first, but she also gets to undo her first sin as a demi-god when she told Adam to "eat this" (Gen 3:6), by preaching the truth to Adam (Jesus' disciples), of who the real God is and that He has risen as He said He would!

Remember the parable of the workers in the field (Mat 20:1-16)? This life has been a long road for Adam and Eve and we still have a little way to go until we all are again standing in front of the Tree of Life to take freely of it (Rev 22:2). However, it is time for Eve to stand up, in this last hour and take her rightful place beside Adam. One would think a statement like this would generate celebration but Eve will still have to manage her command from God to be submissive against standing in a place where Adam may not believe she deserves to be. It is also possible that some Eves will not want to accept this responsibility. These Eves will just want equal rights.

Also, like the workers in the field, in that parable, that worked through the heat of the day and carried out most of the hard labor, Adam will expect to receive more from God when she is placed at his side to become equal to him in this last hour. For she that made herself first became last and now she that is last, God will make first (Mat 19:30). Expect these feelings to garner strife but also expect the lack of these feelings from Adam to demonstrate the Holy Spirit working in him. For Jesus said that we will know them by their fruits (Mat 7:16).

B. WHY (TO BE WHOLE, OF COURSE)

Again, why must God restore Eve? It's enough to believe God will restore her just because His Word will not return to Him void. In other words, He made them two, male and female as a unit in Him, He will receive them back, male and female, in the same unified way He made them. The beginning is also the ending. The Alpha and Omega. The three are one. The representation of His body as They said, "let us make man after our image, after our likenesses," (Genesis 1:26). Just as we start out in the garden with the tree of life, we end in Revelations with the tree of Life and God saying "Let whosoever will come" (Rev 22:17). So, God will restore Eve to her rightful place so they two can be whole, of course.

In Isaiah, where God declares that He is not mad at us anymore because He Himself by His arm has rough salvation and comforted us, both male and female (Isa 12:1). This He did through Jesus' sacrifice. Also, the words Jesus spoke to the woman caught in the act of adultery comes the mind (John 8:11). Jesus is saying this specifically to Eve after He justifies her; 'where are your accusers...then neither do I condemn you.'

Because we ate from the Tree of knowledge of good and evil, we approach this with the attitude of needing proof or knowledge to know. God understands this, so he gives us a trail to follow that leads us to a conclusion that is based in His Word. Remember, I said if I cannot give you scripture for the basis of my conclusions, it's not truth or proof; neither should you believe my words to be anything more than my opinion in this instance. However, if I can show you this thread in the scriptures, this should warrant your attention; to prove to yourself, at the very least, if the scriptures say these things or not.

If someone handed you a one-hundred-dollar bill and it had no image on the back, what would you think? I know the first thing I would think is that it is a fake or counterfeit. If I knew enough to know that the bill should have a front and back side to it with a distinctive image on both sides, and it didn't, I certainly would not accept it or try to use it as currency. Yet we know Adam and Eve started out as two halves of a whole (male and female, created He them, Gen 1:27) but we are willing to accept one half as the whole. Could understanding this, as not a part of our reality, in the lives we live, be the beginning of understanding true unity, as God defines unity?

What does God say about unity (John 17)? What examples are in the Bible that concern two of anything? Could these examples be part of the subtle meaning that makes up the story of the original two, Adam and Eve? From Jewish tradition, the definition of a friend is two bodies with one soul. I haven't tracked down how long ago this saying became a part of their ideology for the meaning of friendship but as the holders of the Oracles of God (Rom 3:2), one would have to believe it sprang from their understanding of unity through God's Word.

It seems to be that the master plan of God is to be one with His creation at a level where the creation gets to choose to be a part of God. I Corinthians 15:28 talks about God being all in all at the end of this whole narrative or story that we are living out. To go through the trouble to divide life to create a unity that was initially there must mean that something was missing that God wanted. Could it be as simple as God wanting individuals with His capabilities, with the gift of thought or self-awareness, that could choose to love him back? Could it be this simple? If so, what would be the cost of creating this avenue? Obviously, the creation could choose not to love him. This choice, not to love Him, would produce a flow of energy that would be opposite to the energy coming from God. Since God can only be who He is, He would have to create layers of existence where He is not, in order to create a vacuum to allow that part of the creation that did not choose to love Him, to exist. Perhaps, this is where the creation of development comes into play. This is why time exists for us because God is not willing that any should perish (2 Peter 3:9). The very nature of God would give us time to choose. However, God would respect our decision in the end which would give us the concept of Hell. A place where the presence of God is not.

How does God get across to us that all life is important? We tend to think if God is doing something and something goes wrong, He can just wipe it out and start over again with no real consequences. Although God can start over, nowhere in the Bible does it imply that there are no consequences to an action like this even at God's level of being. The greatest proof of this is what it cost Jesus to redeem us. There was risk there (note the 'if' in this statement by Jesus in John 12:32) and it cost Jesus more than we can fathom.

C. A THREEFOLD CORD IS HARDLY BROKEN

Remember that Jesus said, "to whom much is forgiven, loves much" (Luke 7:47). Well, think of this in relation to the different heights Adam fell versus Eve. She fell further. She had to not only acknowledge her sin, as Adam has too, but also acknowledge that she set the events we live in into motion. Because of this, God had to turn His back to her and put her face in the dust of submission, like God put the serpent's face in the dirt (Gen 3:14) until the Seed should come, after which God restores her to her place. She endures this with a knowing or understanding that Adam lacked. She has to know that God is forgiving her much more than him in order to appreciate or 'love much' as Jesus said.

When this repentance occurs, she that was made last becomes first and he that was first becomes last; not as a punishment but in the process of the restoration. Why is this necessary? We must look at what the scriptures say about what must happen in the end-times to conclude this narrative or story. Is she needed in a way that she could not participate before because of sin; before the Seed came?

What would the story look like if the women

had not gone to the tomb? When would the disciples become aware that Jesus rose? Would it had been when He appeared to them in the closed room (John 20:19)? Think about certain stories in the Bible where women are prominent and remove them. What would have happened without them? I can say here the same thing I have been saying throughout the book; that is that God can make the story or event come out any way He wants using any one He wants. However, if God excludes women in the strange and pivotal stories, Eve would have to ask the question, "who and what am I"? When God includes her in these subtle ways, she gets a hint of who she is. She is flesh of his flesh and bone of his bone (Gen 2:23; Eph 5:30). So, it is only reasonable that after God's redemptive work, she would become in a more obvious way, what Adam is to God and what she is to Adam.

The scriptures say in the last days that God will "pour out His spirit on all flesh; and your sons and daughters shall prophesy..." (Joel 2:28, Act 2:17, 18). As I said before, God always leaves Himself a witness that He includes Eve with subtly. If she were not an important part of His plan, God could have just said in this scripture that your sons will prophesy. God could not leave her out because Adam can't complete God's plan for his life without her any more than Eve can become complete without Adam. In the next verse of Joel 2:29, God repeats Himself in a way that makes it clear that when He says 'all flesh," He means all His people of all social levels and both sexes. When God repeats Himself, this demonstrates that what is being said is not a passing thought. It will happen. It needs to happen to complete the plan.

Why is this important? Without Eve, Adam is alone. Do you remember what God says about man being alone (Gen 2:18)? Let's take a look at Ecclesiastes 4:9-12. This talks about the practical reason to be a twosome. This scripture says two gives each other purpose in life. Also, if one is sick or falls short in some way, the other will help make the situation better (Rom 13:8). If one is ever chilled to the bone, the other is there to help make warmth (James 2:16). Finally, if one is attacked, the other is there to help fend off the attack (Gal 6:1). I invite you to view these aspects of being a twosome in a more spiritual light. How deep does the meaning become for Adam and Eve! Moreover, when we add the Holy Spirit to this mix, we have a trinity of sorts. As Ecclesiastes says, "a threefold cord is not quickly broken" (4:12).

CHAPTER V

STANDING IN OMEGA

A. FOR HE HAS MADE US KINGS AND PRIESTS

So, what is the end of these things? The overarching idea is that if the first fruit is holy then the lump is also holy: and if the root be holy, so are the branches (I Cor 15:20, Rom 11:16). Eve is both part of the first fruit and the branches (Mat 19:6). If therefore Jesus being made a high priest after the order of Melchizedek is the inheritance of Adam as part of the firstfruits, then Eve too inherits this as a part of Adam, (Gen 2:23). So Eve is also a high priest after the order of Melchizedek. For Jesus said himself, "the disciple is not above his master: but every one that is perfect shall be AS his master" (Luke 6:40).

What does this look like for Eve? As I said before, we must ask ourselves what Eve was supposed to be doing relative to Adam before the fall? Was her only job to bear children and help Adam? While they are equal, they do not have the same responsibilities. The best way to understand what Eve should have been is to note how Eve is restricted in the patriarchy and to look at what Jesus restores to her in his coming. Remember when I said that to balance this sin condition, God would have to create a system that would suppress the evil yet augment the good that remained without systemically hurting Adam or Eve? While it might not feel like it, the current system we experience is just that. As we move towards the reign of Jesus, our system of governance will blow apart because it is based in sin. God will pull back His hand to allow our dispensation of governments of man to show everyone and anyone watching what the end of it will be because it is contrary to God's system of governance. Before the obvious ending occurs, God will intervene for the elect's sake (Mat 24:22).

Let's be reminded of what Galatians says, "there is neither Jew nor Greek, there is neither bond nor free, there is neither male nor female: for ye are all one in Christ Jesus" (Gal 3:28). Did you catch it? All these division listed by Paul go from the singular towards the plural; from the first towards the last. The Alpha towards the Omega. Understanding this and studying the Bible this way, one begins to understand the intention of God to make all unified or one again. It becomes very clear what God is doing for Eve when viewed from this perspective.

Let's view this from the opposite side of the gender coin. There are a few symbolisms, in the Bible, that encapsulate the female experience such as being a bride. To my astonishment, when these things are preached, somehow, they are devoid of the femininity and made to make sense in the view of the patriarchy. For example, the Bride of Christ is based on a female point of view since Christ is the Bridegroom; we the Church have to be the fullness of the woman, the bride. Have you ever asked a man how he feels about being a bride? I don't recommend doing this. All the ones I asked got really mad. From this you can observe that Eve can listen to male oriented preaching and not feel excluded. Adam cannot without the help of the Holy Spirit. However, it is high time that they both accept their roles in Christ after the order of Melchizedek. It is time that we are able to accept the meat of the Word (I Cor 3:2). Jesus said that we can do nothing without Him (John 15:5) but the scriptures say that His wife (the Bride) has made Herself ready (Rev 19:7). This is the instant of oneness where She becomes Jesus, Himself because she is able to make HERSELF ready.

So, throughout all this, the one thing I have not mentioned that God told me is that this showering upon all women at the end of time so Eve can take her rightful place, is upon all Eves regardless of belief. Just as the sun rise on the evil and on the good and it rains on the just and on the unjust (Mat 5:45), this showering from the Holy Spirit will rain upon all women. The ones that embrace the Way, the Truth, the Life will have this special blessing remain on them to progress us further towards the Omega. To be whole again.

B. WHAT IS HE MAKING

We know that God intended for both Adams to be God (Gen 1:26) but in His timing. So, what Satan said to Eve had a ring of truth to it but lacked the truth of God in it. Jesus confirmed this when He confronted the Pharisees as they accused Him of blasphemy for calling Himself the son of God (John 10:33-36). God is not only telling a story through Adam but He is also reproducing Himself.

The sin of Adam was taking on this privilege without God's blessing; outside of God's timing. These six thousand years have been a continual display of what happens when we act outside of God's will.

On the flip side, we learn that there is nothing too hard for the Lord (Gen 18:14). He manages to get us out of all our troubles (Psa. 34:17) and restore us. However, we end up with more blessing than if the brokenness from sin had never happened. We all know that God preferred that we had not experienced this sin walk to Godhood but we did and as I said before, we seem to gain more from God thru this way. Could this be a way to fathom what Jesus' sacrifice cost him? Our increase through an obvious loss is proportional to Jesus's loss for our increase. I suspect that it is greater than we can understand at the present but we will have an opportunity to understand in the future days of glory.

With all that Jesus sacrificed, is it such a

strange thing that Eve too would be made a priest after the of Melchizedek? God, who so freely gave His Son for us, would not deny anything from us (John 3:16)? Especially a transitory title that will go away when God creates a new heaven and a new earth (I Cor 15:24, 28).

To commune with love, one must also be love. God is Love.

C. THE CONCLUSION OF ALL THINGS

So, we Come full circle. Just as knowledge was used to harm mankind, then knowledge was used to restore mankind, Eve was used to destroy man's connection with God, she is used to restore our connection to God. The emphasis is not on Eve but rather on God's ability to use instruments that were perverted to harm us, to restore us back to Him with greater blessings. This shows that our God is truly the God of Gods and King of Kings and Lord of Lords.

I ask you again, who will you choose? Who will be God in your life? Yourself or the one true God.

Which way will you choose?
Which Eve are you?

THE END

EPILOGUE

I hope this book enlightens you and inspires you to do your own research. I hope you will look with new understanding on how women are used in God's plan. God did not just throw her away because she sinned or because she sinned first.

I know this revelation has enlightened me and has made me see that there are more depths to the Bible than we know; some correlations that I have never made until God told me what I have just shared with you about Eve. If God wills, and when the time is right, perhaps He will let me write another book. That one, in the spirit of God being all things to all people, (I Cor 9:22, Heb 2:17) will be entitled, "Jesus the Man, Jesus the Woman."

May Jesus empower you to be the woman He meant you to be!

DEAR READER

The intent of this book is for us to gain the unity or oneness that God desires for us. We are all well aware that this unity will come by great personal sacrifice because the offer that gave us the choice to be one with God came by great personal sacrifice from God; the offering of his son.

Therefore, I encourage you to press in and take it by force, by the True Way and the Only Way.

God Bless!

ABOUT THE AUTHOR

Ellen Ward was born in Philadelphia, PA and moved to her parents' birthplace, Virginia, as a teenager. She attended Christopher Newport University in Newport News, VA and earned a degree in Philosophy and Religious Studies. She accepted a job in the government where she currently works.

ACKNOWLEDGEMENTS

I would like to thank all the women who came before me that pushed through the social and religious mores that have allowed me the choice to be more than a wife or mother, without denigrating the women who chose to be wives or mothers by the standards of the social norms.